Dim-Mak

Advanced

The Finer Points of Death-Point Striking

Erle Montaigue

Paladin Press
Boulder, Colorado

Also by Erle Montaigue:

Baguazhang: Fighting Secrets of the Eight Trigram Palms

Dim-Mak: Death-Point Striking

Dim-Mak's 12 Most Deadly Katas: Points of No Return

Power Taiji

Secrets of Dim-Mak: An Instructional Video (video)

The Encyclopedia of Dim-Mak: The Main Meridians

The Encyclopedia of Dim-Mak:
    The Extra Meridians, Points, and More

Ultimate Dim-Mak: How to Fight a Grappler and Win

Precise anatomical point locations are taken from the *Point Location and Point Dynamics Manual* by Carole and Cameron Rogers. If you would like to obtain a copy, please write to us at P.O. Box 792, Murwillumbah NSW 2484, Australia. All of the topics discussed in the individual chapters of this book are covered in further detail on video. Videotapes focusing on specific areas of interest are available from MTG video at the above address.

Advanced Dim-Mak:
The Finer Points of Death-Point Striking
by Erle Montaigue

Copyright © 1994 by Erle Montaigue

ISBN 0-87364-779-3
Printed in the United States of America

Published by Paladin Press, a division of
Paladin Enterprises, Inc.
Gunbarrel Tech Center
7077 Winchester Circle
Boulder, Colorado 80301 USA
+1.303.443.7250

Direct inquiries and/or orders to the above address.

PALADIN, PALADIN PRESS, and the "horse head" design
are trademarks belonging to Paladin Enterprises and
registered in the United States Patent and Trademark Office.

All rights reserved. Except for use in a review, no
portion of this book may be reproduced in any form
without the express written permission of the publisher.

Neither the author nor the publisher assumes
any responsibility for the use or misuse of
information contained in this book.

Visit our Web site at www.paladin-press.com

Contents

Warning

The techniques and drills depicted in this book are extremely dangerous. It is not the intent of the author or publisher to encourage readers to attempt any of these techniques and drills without proper professional supervision and training. Attempting to do so can result in severe injury or death. Do not attempt any of these techniques or drills without the supervision of a certified instructor.

The author, publisher, and distributors of this book disclaim any liability from any damage or injuries of any type that a reader or user of information contained within this book may encounter from the use of said information. *This book is for information purposes only.*

Foreword

As a practitioner of the so-called hard and external art of karate-do, I found my initial training was very hard—lots of physical work and fighting (in other words, lots of sweat and pain!). In free-fighting, while we, the junior grades, had to control our attacks to the face and head (although we were allowed to hit the body as hard as we could), the senior grades often did not attempt to control their attacks toward our faces and heads. So in the end we became quite good at ducks and head-slips, etc. But even so, most of my colleagues have false front teeth and somewhat deformed noses. I consider myself one of the lucky ones—I have my original set of teeth (although chipped) and a straight nose.

Our aims of daily practice were (and still are) as follows:

1) to cultivate strong fighting spirit (never retreat, always go forward)
2) to develop great hitting power—knock the opponent down with one strike if possible

3) to learn to defend ourselves properly so that we do not get hit while we hit the opponent

4) to strengthen our bodies so that we can absorb attacks in case we get hit

In order to achieve our first aim, we often had to fight in front of a wall so that we could not physically retreat. This way, we learned to go forward to block and counterattack when attacked. Toward our fourth aim, we did lots of physical exercises to strengthen our bodies—500 to 1,000 sit-ups daily was the norm, and our record of nonstop sit-ups was 2,500!

As our study progressed, we started to learn a few things, i.e., proper traditional karate teachings. With sanchin practice, we learned correct posture, proper fixation of body, and most importantly, proper breathing. Correct breathing will increase internal abdominal pressure and make the body like an inflated tire. If one likens a well-trained abdominal muscle to a high-quality tire, it is not usable if it is not inflated first. As you keep practicing this, eventually you become able to take quite a hard blow without much physical effort by just keeping good internal air pressure.

We also learned that big dynamic movements with lots of physical effort are not really necessary to deliver powerful techniques. When one keeps one's center to the lower abdomen (*tanden* or *tan-tien*), with correct posture and proper breathing, small, seemingly effortless techniques can be very powerful.

So we karate-kas (karate people) progress from external to internal and from hardness to softness until external and internal harmonize and hardness and softness complement each other. Each seemingly hard technique must contain an element of softness within and vice versa.

This same process takes place in every Japanese martial art.

A gentle cut of a kendo master has a devastating effect when it connects. The muscles of the arms and shoulders of a kyudo (Japanese archery) master are completely soft and relaxed while pulling bow and arrow. Each martial art has a different application, but the underlying principles are the same. The three most important words within Japanese martial arts are *shisei* (posture), *kokyu* (breathing), and *hara,* or *tanden.*

My first encounter with taiji (t'ai chi) was in 1978 while living in Brussels. I met a Chinese gentleman, Mr. Kuo, who had been a student of Master Wong in Taiwan. He was 78 years old and told me he had been practicing taiji for 51 years without missing a single day. His most impressive attributes were his health and vigor. Since then, I have met several taiji practitioners, all of them practicing for their health. And one cannot deny that they are getting great benefit from it.

But taiji cannot be complete *as a martial art* without some hard aspects. In saying this, I am not trying to undermine taiji, as there are many karate-kas in the world who never progressed from the basic hard, external level, and thus their art is not complete.

Erle Montaigue, the author, and I both have the same years of age and the same years of martial arts practice, although our paths did not cross until recent years. When I attended his seminar for the first time, I was pleasantly surprised that he was actually teaching a fighting method. Another nice surprise was that his taiji has lots of common points with *our* karate. I was impressed by his vast knowledge of martial arts and particularly of vital points, or *dim-mak.*

He is one of the rare, lucky people who learned "the real thing" from true masters of the art. I also must point out that, despite his lighthearted approach, he has a strong moral standard and balanced view, which is also a sign of the true martial artist. Moreover, he is a very generous person, as he gladly passes on the valuable information he got through hard work to anybody who is keen to learn through various seminars, videos, and books.

His first book on the subject of dim-mak, *Dim-Mak:*

Death-Point Striking, was by far the most comprehensive work on this subject among several books I have seen. And now he has completed this second volume on the subject, which will enlighten readers even further on the subject of dim-mak.

Although he explains the art of dim-mak from the point of view of taiji (he cannot help it, as he is, after all, a taiji master), I believe this book will benefit greatly all serious martial artists, irrespective of discipline or style, and give them a healthy respect for the art of taiji.

Thus, I wholeheartedly recommend this fine work to everyone.

Keiji Tomiyama,
Senior Instructor
6th Dan, Shito-ryu Karate-do Kofukan
(International)

Preface

"I have come to where I am now, armed with only the knowledge of how little I know."

—Sidney Poitier

The art of dim-mak is a complex one, consisting of many different facets. I discussed a number of these in my earlier book, *Dim-Mak: Death-Point Striking*. In this book I cover areas of training, points, revival, and healing in particular that I did not include in the first book. I am also including a section in Chapter 4 on street survival using the simplest of dim-mak methods—those that do not require you to invest years of study and practice in order to attain a high level of expertise. You can learn these most deadly methods in a matter of hours.

However, reaching a high level of proficiency in the more advanced methods of dim-mak does take some time and much more practice. According to an old Chinese saying, "It takes three lifetimes to learn dim-mak." This does not refer to learning at a very basic level, but rather at a very high level, and is a way of saying that it is a long, hard road to gaining this advanced proficiency. But with the training provided in this and my last book on the subject, the goal is not unobtainable.

A little dedication, many hours of practice, a few bruises, and you will begin to see why many of the world's leading martial artists are now turning to dim-mak. They are finding that it not only gives their own martial art a new dimension, it also gives them some insight into what their own style was like before it became watered down as a result of so-called masters simply not giving out certain information (either because they wanted to hide it or they simply didn't know it). They are finding that there is a wealth of information to be gained, not only in the fighting art but also in the healing art.

Acknowledgments

Thanks and acknowledgments go to the following people:

Sandra, the beautiful,

Ben, the beautiful,

Eli, the beautiful,

Kataleena, the beautiful,

Erland, the beautiful,

Kristian, the beautiful,

Shantel, the beautiful (grand-daughter) . . .

without whom I would not be Erle Montaigue.

My students worldwide, far too many to list here, without whom I would know very little, with a special mention to the Norwegian lot, including all of my students in Scandinavia. And to the Sunday class, for causing me to like teaching basics again.

Ken Johnson, for his enthusiasm and support in running the WTBA in Scandinavia.

Jim Uglow, for his support in running the WTBA in London.

Al Krych, head of the WTBA in the United States, for his support and the Foreword to Chapter 6.

Mike Babin, head of the WTBA in Canada, for his support.

Bill Barnes (my old wrestling partner), head of WTBA in Manchester, for his support.

Annie, Deb, Lyn, and Glenn in New Zealand, WTBA reps.

Keiji Tomiyama, for his support and the Foreword to this book.

Slavo Gozdzik, for his support.

Jim Marincic, for trying to hit me and keeping me on my toes.

John Ross, a bloody nice bloke and head of WTBA Perth.

Steve Bloom, our representative in Fredrikstadt, Norway.

Bruce Armstrong, even though he is a Kyokushin warrior.

Allen Bracken, for being one of my first training partners and from whom I learned heaps.

Les Anwyl, for sticking with me since the beginning.

Jeni Blake, for also sticking with me from the start.

Axel Post and Steve Dunn, for also sticking with me all along.

For helping out and being in the photos, Stuart, Peter, Jim, and Wal.

Kevin Brennan, for making me famous, and for being a fine friend and mentor where journalism and yaks are concerned.

Terry O'Neil, also for making me famous and for his friendship.

Graham Noble, for his support.

Mike Sigman for his support, even though it sometimes made him not so liked by some.

Bill and Charmaine, for being great Aussies.

Ruth, my sister-in-law, for being so good to look at. Jenny, my sister-in-law, for teaching me much. Dianne, my sister-in-law, for teaching the children so much. Marge, for being my arguing partner and a really nice person. Arthur, for teaching me so much about dogs and birds.

Aaron Beth'el, for so much love and for authoring wonderful books.

Chris Madden, for teaching me so much about Chinese medicine.

Ruth Galene, for showing me that one just goes on forever.

Rolly Brown, for playing great music with me.

Cheryl Ann, for being my first wife and mother of my first two boys.

Thanks again to Karen Pochert with Paladin, who showed me so much as far as authoring is concerned.

In memory of: Steve Hurst (1992), Jenny Brennan (1993), Albert Hescot (1988), Shane Brown (1992), Chang Yiu-chun (1987), Margaret Kathleen (1985), and Charles Montaigue (1987).

The Demise of Taijiquan

My goal has always been to present taiji as the deadly fighting system that it really is, as opposed to being just a bunch of slow movements with little or no resemblance to a self-defense system. This book is just one method by which I am trying to tell the truth about this great fighting art. But the going is not easy. There is much resistance, and it comes from the taiji people themselves—those who believe they can defend themselves without getting their hands dirty or actually having to fight! It's most unfortunate that most people in the taiji area are not martial artists. For the most part, taiji instructors (bar a few) have this mystical idea that they will be able to move objects with their qi, or energy, and not actually have to defend themselves physically. The karate people who take up taiji do not have this way of thinking. They see what I am presenting and take it for what it is, whereas many of the "taiji" people think that what I present is too brutal.

It's not a very kind world nowadays, and brutal methods, I'm afraid, are necessary to survival, just as they were way back in the fourteenth century when Chang Sang-feng invented this art, which was then known simply as dim-mak, or death-point striking.

Chang invented this art as a means of defense against others who would kill him or his family. He needed some way of teaching his family this deadly information he had discovered, without allowing others who would harm them to gain it. So he invented a series of slow, dancelike movements that resembled only vaguely a self-defense art. Some of them looked like self-defense movements, but only on a very basic level. All of the more deadly point strikes, including the locations, the correct directions, and the proper amounts of pressure, were hidden within this dance. Only Chang's most loyal and trusted family members and students learned the real meanings of the forms. Often these were as seemingly insignificant and innocuous as a finger movement—something so small that anyone looking on as the form was being performed would not see it. But Chang's students learned what each tiny movement represented.

Chang taught a handful of students, who in turn would teach only one or two trusted students. One of these select few was a man called Wang Tsung-yeuh, who was a scholar. Wang decided to write down what Chang had taught him but to include only the movements from the forms and not what they meant. The meanings he left to direct transmission from teacher to student.

One of Wang's students, Zhiang, visited the Chen Village (Chen Chiago). The Chens were a well-known family of martial artists and were practicing what is now known as Shao-lin boxing, handed down by monks who lived at the Shao-lin Temple (Little Forest Temple). Also at this time, a man called Yang Lu-ch'an (who had inveigled his way into the village when the Chens discovered him sleeping on their doorstep in the freezing cold and almost dying) was living there and working as a cleaner. Zhiang and Yang became friends, and Zhiang eventually taught Yang the martial art of dim-mak. Yang had been studying the Chens' martial arts, but he became so good at this new art that his prowess eclipsed that of even the most senior of the Chen masters.

Yang left the village and later married and had his own family. He continued to work on his martial art, which he called hao ch'uan, or loose boxing, because of the way the forms were performed, like a rag doll. Later, Yang's grandson Yang Cheng-fu, who inherited the style from his father, Yang Kin-hou (also spelled *Chien-hou*), would form his own style, leaving out many of the more deadly hidden movements (this is roughly the slow-moving style of taiji we now see in the parks in China). Yang Shou-hou, the brother of Yang Cheng-fu, never taught anything but the original style. To my knowledge, he only ever took on three students, and he taught them everything. One of these was Chang Yiu-chun, my main teacher.

It was not until the later part of the nineteenth century that hao ch'uan became "taijiquan." One of the Wu family (founders of another branch of taiji that is one of four main styles today) gave it that name when he learned some of the secret moves from the old dim-mak and decided that the art he had been taught was "the supreme ultimate boxing," which is what taijiquan means. (The Wu family originated with a man called Wu Chien ch'uan [1870–1942], son of Quan-yu [1834–1902]. They were Manchus and, as such, had no surname. Quan-yu adopted the surname of Wu in order to learn from Yang Lu-ch'an [1799-1872], in the latter part of the nineteenth century. His son, Wu Chien-chu'an, kept the Wu name and changed what his father had taught him to for his own style of taiji, now known as the Wu style.)

So it's ironic that the art most people call taiji has now been reduced to a wimp's boxing rather than the "supreme ultimate boxing." Once it was known as the most deadly fighting art ever invented. In Yang Lu-ch'an's time, most other stylists in China looked upon him and the art he had founded as supreme in the martial arts area. Many were jealous of the Yang family and plotted to kill them for fear that they would one day have to use their own styles to prove themselves against these warriors.

So what happened? Nowadays, most other martial artists and even ordinary streetfighters are able to take on any of the so-called taiji masters and grand masters and defeat them with no trouble at all. Most of these taiji people would have no hope of defending themselves in the streets. The reason? Taiji has lost its roots, its beginnings. What people teach as being representative of the whole art today is only a mere shell of taiji's former glory. Most masters from China and in the West ignore even the crucial exercises of small and large san-sau, preferring to teach only the slow form and, at the most, some ineffectual "push hands," which itself has come to hold nothing of its former meaning. Most people who practice the art now are not martial artists. They are people who do not wish to actually fight to defend themselves. Most dismiss the original purpose of taiji, that of self-defense. The reason for this is that modern taiji cannot be used for self-defense, and few, if any, modern masters even know how to teach it for self-defense any longer.

Taiji started out on top of the martial arts heap, and now it is on the bottom, due mainly to one man, Yang Cheng-fu! When he changed his father's form, he rang the death knoll for taiji as a self-defense art. *His* changes were not too bad; they at least left the internal essence intact, even if the physical attributes were greatly diminished. But from that point on it became easier to change the art again and again. Yang Cheng-fu's heart was good, and he had only the best of reasons for making the changes he did. For one, he decided that the art, as it was, was still too close to the original dim-mak, and so he further hid the deadly movements. Also, one of Yang's dreams was to help his people rise up against the many other countries that had invaded China by that time. He knew of the great health benefits that taiji could impart and wanted all Chinese people to gain robust bodies and minds. But the original forms of his grandfather consisted of many movements that would be too difficult for older people of failing health to perform. So Yang modified them, leaving out all of the more strenuous movements.

It was Yang's students who took over when he died—many who weren't even favorite students and some who had only spent some six months at his school—who actually pulled the trigger and killed taiji as a self-defense art by only ever practicing his "modified" form of Yang style. These students went on to change Yang Cheng-fu's form further, leaving the style with little or no internal essence.

Nowadays, many regard this watered-down system as *the* one and only Yang style, denying the very existence of the original Yang style. And so few martial artists take up this form of taiji that what little *was* left of the original fighting art is not being passed on, because martial artists no longer care to know about it.

Many of the American and American/Chinese "masters" and "grand masters" now actually teach Western boxing skills to prop up their useless taiji arts. Some use Western wrestling skills; others rely upon tournament push hands. Still others resort to trickery to make us believe that because they are not able to defend themselves using their own bodies, they are able to move people without touching them, etc. It is only because they are so unsure of their own abilities that they must resort to these circus tricks. These people know that they are able to fool many people time after time and still have classes of 200 and 300 people who never even think of questioning what the instructor is teaching them.

At a recent seminar in the capital state of Australia, the so-called leader of the Yang family from China actually stated that one of the secrets of taiji was not to do it (the form) when wearing a short-sleeved shirt! The reason? Because one loses one's qi out of one's arms if one does not wear a long-sleeved shirt! What are we, stupid?! Many of the 400 attendees left halfway through this seminar, but most did not even think to question this statement. (Karate people laugh at this kind of thing, and it makes the art that I teach look bloody stupid!)

One of the main reasons taiji is not being taught in its truest form is that back in the early part of this century there was a meeting between all of the greatest masters of taiji. They decided that enough was enough; no more outsiders would be given the family secrets. All of those present, who represented all of the major styles of taiji at that time, agreed to teach only the real thing to a handful of either family members or a select few of the most dedicated outsiders. To others, they decided they would teach only a watered-down version (to the point where some of them even invented new styles in a further effort to hide the original). They were all bound to this secrecy, and they went their ways and taught many students, but only the watered-down versions. What these masters did not know was that in years to come, even the Chinese masters would only practice the watered-down forms, such as that which Yang Cheng-fu invented.

Luckily, there are still a few—only a few—who still know the art of Yang Cheng-fu's brother Yang Shou-hou, who did not change the style. These are the ones who refused to go along with the plan to keep the original system from outsiders by only teaching the very basics. We know that taiji, or hao ch'uan, as it was called before this century, is the greatest of all fighting arts, but we must distinguish between what Yang Cheng-fu taught and what his brother taught, and his father before him, and his father before him.

There are two distinct Yang-style taiji methods now. One is the most common Yang Cheng-fu form, from whence the Cheng Man-ching style comes; the other is the original Yang style of Yang Lu-ch'an—the *only* one that can rightfully be called this style. In fact, if Yang came back today, firstly, he would not even know what we were talking about when we said "taijiquan," or "supreme ultimate boxing." He would say, "please teach me." Yang Lu-ch'an did not invent taijiquan; he founded Yang-style hao ch'uan, or loose boxing, an offshoot of the original art of Chang Sang-feng, which was dim-mak or death-point striking.

Many years ago, I predicted that in China there would be no one left who would know about the real fighting art of taiji. And I believe that this has come true. Mainly because of the Chinese people wanting to win at tournaments now, we have seen what was once a great self-defense art become an acrobatic art with absolutely no internality about it. And those who were in the know have either died or have moved to the West, where they are not teaching anyone anyway. Now it is we in the West who must preserve the original taiji or hao ch'uan art.

Unfortunately, we also see these silly push-hands tournaments in the West now as well, mainly in the United States. The rationale is that they engender interest and bring many more practitioners. This is exactly what happened to taiji at the beginning of this century. Yang Cheng-fu made it more accessible to the general public by changing it so that it became relatively easy to learn, and now we have nothing. The tournaments have ruined taiji. When there is competition, the art is lost. It becomes purely a physical exercise to "look good" for the judges so that we can claim to be better than someone else! That's great Taoism, isn't it? If you *must* have tournaments, get in there and beat the shit out of each other, and then you can claim to at least be a better fighter than your opponent, but let's not place this undue attention upon push hands. Taiji is an internal art, and no one is able to see what is inside of you. They can only judge the physical movements. I learned long ago that physical movements mean nothing.

Also, there have also been many mistranslations from Chinese into English. Some were simple mistakes, while others were purposely proliferated by the Chinese to prevent outsiders from gaining their secrets. Taiji, for instance, is not soft! You cannot have a "soft" fighting art. You can have a "soft" martial art, but that's what it stays as forevermore—just a martial art, and not a self-defense or fighting art. The *correct* word to describe taiji is "loose." *Fa-jing* means "explosive energy." And when one learns about fa-jing or "loose boxing," one understands that the power generated by this loose body is immense.

So taiji has come to a bunch of self-centered individuals who know human nature dictates that a person will take the easy way out every time. They have changed what was once great but difficult to obtain and made it small and easy to obtain. It all began when Yang Cheng-fu decided to change the original to make it easier for us on the one hand and on the other to hide it from outsiders so that the art would remain as "the family jewel." From then on it all went downhill.

Fortunately, there are still those who believe in hard work and who follow the ways of the original Yang system. And as more and more real martial artists get onto this martial art, perhaps we will see a resurgence—something that was once great will begin making its mark again.

I hold workshops all over the world, barely breaking even, so that people will see taiji for what it used to be. Not that I am any great warrior, but at least I have learned what I believe to be the original art of Yang Shou-hou from his student Chang Yiu-chun. My hope is that all martial artists will see taiji for what it is, a great fighting system.

As I mentioned earlier, the "taiji" people who attend my workshops (mainly in the United States) are really put off by the idea that they must actually fight to defend themselves. Actually, not all of them feel this way. I have some excellent students in Canada and the United States (like Mike Babin and Al Krych, my reps in those countries, respectively, as well as many others). But the difference is that they have done some other styles; they were martial artists before I got to them. The purely "taiji" people, on the other hand, those who do not wish to "get their hands dirty," think I'm some sort of animal! (Me! Come on, now. I have a big snake in my old dairy shed on my farm, and he loves me!)

Self-defense is not pretty; it is not easy. It is ugly. And ugly methods are required to successfully defend against ugly people. There is no easy way, nor is there any way to put someone down without hurting him, save for maybe a drunk in a pub. Against the person who is really trying to get you, you really have to use dire methods to defend yourself, and it is not pretty.

So nowadays, I tend to give workshops to either my own instructors and their students or to whole groups of karate people who wish to get back to their roots. I do not usually give workshops to other taiji groups, as I do not like scaring people, and contrary to those who would think otherwise, I am a peace-loving family man who simply happens to have a very real idea of what it's like out there in the streets, in addition to a very real understanding of my own martial art and ability.

Karate people know about martial arts, and they are able to pick out the bullshit. Karateka (karate practitioners) are usually good, honest people, and when they see something that is good, they take it. But if it is not so, then they leave it. When I use the word karateka, I mean dedicated martial artists who have attained their rank due to many years of hard work, and not those who have obtained their black belts and dan rankings over a period of 10 years or so.

That's the downside of karate. So many teachers reach a certain degree and then break away from their teachers to form their own systems. They then either grade themselves up or have their students do it for them. I have seen people who have only ever attained the degree of brown belt in one system break away and then grade themselves to black belt, 6th dan! This is happening all around the world. And being good, honest people, interested only in their own system and doing well in it, those who *are* real karateka usually do not come out publicly against such practices, not wishing to draw attention to the fact that these types exist in the business.

I had a chap here in Australia who had obtained the degree of black belt from a rather "gray" karate teacher. He left that particular teacher and then wanted to be graded up to 5th dan! So he phoned me, asking if I would do it! I refused, but later saw that he was calling himself a 5thdan black belt! He'll probably be up to 8th-dan master by the time this book is published.

But this is the way with lies. All one has to do is to wait! We have seen this many times in the martial arts, with so-called masters claiming that they are the direct descendants of the original styles, and so on. Those in the know just dismiss these people, knowing that they are charlatans, but do nothing about it. As time passes, those in the know either move on or give up their martial arts, and the new people do not know anything about the beginnings of these teachers. So they believe their lies, and eventually, the lies become "truth."

So when I say "internal arts," such as taiji, bagwa and h'sin-i, I'm not referring to 90 percent of what is passed off as being representative of these arts—especially taiji. Because taiji has become so popular over the past 30 or so years, it has lost much of its former greatness because of its mystical side. How can one claim to be teaching a martial or fighting art when it consists of a few slow movements or some push hands? How is it possible to learn each posture from the forms or katas as techniques and then say that this is the martial art of taiji? There has to be something more to it than that. And there is. Read on.

Dim-Mak Ingredients and Training Methods

1

Many people still think that learning dim-mak is a simple matter of learning the points and then going out and hitting them. Wrong.

Sure, many of the points will work no matter who hits them. For instance, Conceptor Vessel (Cv 22), the pit of the neck, is a particularly easy point to strike and will cause great damage no matter how it is hit. Most martial artists know about the pit of the neck and how dangerous it is. But in order to learn dim-mak at its highest level, one must have the correct ingredients to begin with, and this involves a little work.

Most of the dim-mak points will only work if the person hitting them has "internal power," and there are a number of ways to gain this power. Luckily, the Yang family masters of old (from the fourteenth century to about the middle of the eighteenth century) who invented dim-mak and the "internal" systems left us with physical training methods to gain this so-called internal power.

The body is an amazing piece of machinery, and with a lot of training, we are able to make it perform what *seem* to be supernatural feats of strength. Most of this is purely physical, of course, with the body being placed into the absolute correct position to be able to take great weights and attack from no distance at all. But there *is* something else involved here as well, and this, I guess, can be called "qi power." This is the part of taiji, for instance, that is inexplicable, the part for which there is no physical explanation. No one knows where it comes from, and no one is able to call upon it for show or ego; it just comes when you least expect it.

I and many others have experienced this power that is there one second and gone the next. It manifests itself when one's life is threatened or when one needs it most. This *need* can vary according to the person and can lie on a sliding scale anywhere from simply not wishing to look stupid in front of a crowd to facing a life-threatening situation. But, it *is* there, and, given some hard training, it will manifest itself. There are no training methods that will actually give us the ability to call upon this "force" at will, but we can train to have it *manifest itself* automatically when we need it most.

The training methods look simple and *are* simple on a purely physical level. However, in order for us to obtain what the classics (sayings left to us by the Chinese masters of old) tell us we should obtain from these exercises—such as a robust body, a calm mind, great health, a self-defense system unequaled by any other, relaxation of mind and body, and an understanding of the workings of the universe, man, and God—there is much internal work to be done also. This internal work is done with the mind, or rather *not* with the mind. What I mean by this is that the conscious mind is actually doing nothing, nothing at all. The body is moving using its own mind— the internal mind.

Take tennis players out on the court. They do not have to think about hitting the ball. They do not think, as the ball is coming for them, about such and such a vector and angle, the speed of the ball, how fast to move the arm, how much power is needed, and so on. It just becomes instinctive. Such is the power of the mind; there is no computer in existence that can make such calculations in such a short time.

It is the same when we are trying to cultivate "internal power." It's an easy but difficult thing to do: easy in that we simply have to do nothing, difficult in that it is bloody hard to cause the mind to give up its control over the functions of the physical body, bar the automatic functions that keep us alive, such as the heartbeat, respiration, and so on. In most people, the conscious mind is conditioned to cause us to make certain physical movements or reactions. We *think* about doing things other than those that occur on a subconscious level, such as lung, heart, kidney, and liver functions. Through training, we can cause the conscious mind to give up its hold over our physical actions so that we are able to move as we should, subconsciously, when we are attacked, rather than thinking about certain techniques we learned down at the local karate club.

I will be giving you some "simple" exercises that will enable you to gain this internal power—exercises that seem to have nothing to do with strength but really have *all* to do with real power. What we are trying to do is use that immense power of the brain, and, as the body and internal mind are inextricably linked, with what one does affecting the other, these exercises will help you to gain this ability.

THE POST

This exercise, "the post," has come to us from another of the dim-mak arts, bagwazhang (also spelled *pa-kua-chang*). Bagwazhang (bagwa for short) is one of three so-called internal fighting arts founded in China. Taijiquan is one of these, as is h'sin-i ch'uan, or "mind/body" boxing. Bagwazhang is said to be the daughter of taiji, while h'sin-i is said to be the son. The movements of bagwazhang are performed around the circumference of a circle, unlike the more orthodox forms or katas of taiji, which are done in straight lines. There are eight parts to bagwa, and the name means literally "eight diagram palm" because it is based upon the *Chinese Book of Changes,* or the *I Ching,* and uses only the palms for self-defense and attack. It is also an internal art because it makes greater use of the inner mind than the body, although bagwa *is* a little more physical than taiji in the beginning of one's training.

There are three training methods by which to gain the post, which is so named because this is the state of mind we must get into in order to gain internal power and the use of qi. (Video No. MTG54 from MTG Video covers all of the post exercises.) We must become like a post stuck into the ground: still, calm, and balanced, but at the same time be able to move freely. No matter what leg we are standing on or even if we are standing upon two legs, the attitude is the same: it's as if a pole is running from our standing leg up through the backbone and is solidly stuck into the ground. If a force now comes at this post, it simply turns in its hole and spins the force away, not moving backward in doing so. For real-life self-defense situations, this post is one of the most important areas of one's training, and certainly one of the most crucial to dim-mak. This standing and turning will only take a fraction of a second to execute when needed, and it's the turning that gives us the ability to reattack the force as we are negating it.

Most people's idea of yielding is one of having some force come in and allowing it to make contact. Then they take a step backward and turn the waist while grabbing the attacking arm, etc. This does not work in real life; it only works in the dojo or dawgwan (training hall). In real life, you only have that split second to react, and it will be this post training that will hold you in good stead for such attacks.

If, for instance, you were attacked and you did not have the post, you would have to take a solid stance, a low stance, so that the force would not push you backward or over. Using the post, however, you can take the force in any stance, even one that would normally be considered inferior, and still not be disadvantaged. And isn't this the way that fights or attacks occur? You are not given time to get into a strong stance, a la most people's idea of push hands. You are attacked while standing there minding your own business, sitting, walking, or whatever.

So why do most people insist on training with this incredibly difficult low stance, that which most people in the taiji area take to show how strong they are? Is it to make the legs strong? Why? We must be able to defend ourselves with normal legs, not huge football-player legs. We do not wish to spend the rest of our lives training our legs to be strong and big. One such "master" of the Chen-style taiji is very good at taking the low stance so that he cannot be pushed over, but if one looks at his thighs, they are like tree trunks. We mere mortal humans, who must work and play with our kids, and such, do not have the time to invest in such daylong practice. We are lucky to have enough time to be able to practice once per day for an hour or so in the mornings.

So this is where the post training comes in. It is relatively simple—bar the mental aspects—and takes up only a short period of time in actual training. The beauty of these exercises is that you can practice them all the time and no one will even notice you are doing them. There is a formal way of doing these exercises, and people *would* notice this; however, we can modify them so that we do not appear to be doing anything strange.

After some time, this post training becomes your exercise, your meditation, and your *qigong*. (Qigong, covered in Chapter 9, means literally "internal work or breath" and is the oldest of the Chinese breathing exercises.) In the post exercises, we combine certain stances with certain breathing exercises to cause the body to become relaxed so that the qi, or energy, will flow freely to all parts of the body. So much from a few simple steps! Every muscle and tendon in the body is exercised for the martial arts, which in turn affects many of the healing aspects of the body. But the most important effect is on the mind.

The First Post Exercise: Post Preparation

This first exercise cannot be done if you are not using the mind correctly. You can do the movements physically—a ballet dancer would be able to perform them easily. But to do it correctly with the right mental attitude is difficult. A ballet dancer would probably never be able to understand this, because she or he is dealing in purely physical movement, whereas we are dealing with body *and* mind.

Figure 1

Look at Figure 1. This is the beginning posture for each of the post exercises. It's nothing special, just standing there, weight on the rear (in this case right) leg, arms hanging by the sides. Take another look and see how relaxed the arms are. Look also at the shoulders, the head, the back. The "C" back, which I covered in detail in my first book (*Dim-Mak: Death-Point Striking*), is the correct position of the back for the post. This is a way of holding the back (in the shape of a "C," rather than in the normal "S" shape) that brings forth extreme yang energy, or animal attack energy. This position causes us to utilize the part of the brain called the "reptilian brain," which is the ancient human brain, the one reptiles have. It is the survival part of the brain, and while we do not normally use it, we have ways to call it into action when attacked. The body is positioned as if the rear leg is a post, while the front leg can be lifted up at any time without changing the position of the body or shifting of the weight. This is true "post standing."

Figure 2

Figure 3

See how in Figure 2, the front foot is raised without changing the position of the body. Only the absolutely necessary muscles have been used to do this. The arms have not changed; there is no tension in the arms, they still just hang there. The chin is pulled in slightly, causing the backbone to be pulled upward. The tongue is pressed lightly to the hard palate, and the breath is slow and deep without causing any shoulder movement. The breath is going deep down to the middle and lower abdomen, and you are breathing through your nose. If your hand happens to be in the way of your lifting leg, you must not move it but allow the thigh to move the arm as necessary, without any resistance. Be aware of this, as most people will put some tension into the arm when the leg touches it.

You have breathed in. If you wish to stand there for awhile, your tongue must now change from the upper to the lower palate as you breathe out through your mouth (fig. 3). You will hear some sound as you exhale because of the position of the tongue. So when you lift, you breathe in through your nose with the tongue on the upper palate, and when you sink, you breathe out of your mouth with the tongue on the lower palate.

The Second Post Exercise: Stepping Over the Fence

As you lift your left foot as before and breathe in, you imagine that there is a small fence or gate in front of you and you are stepping over it. Remember not to have any other part of your body change position or become tense in any way. You step over the fence, as shown in Figure 4.

As you place your left foot on the ground on the other side of the fence, you breathe out with your tongue now placed on the lower palate just behind the lower teeth ridge. These are the exact same things we must do while performing qigong, which makes this a qigong exercise. Remember, if your hands and arms get in the way, just allow your thigh to move them naturally, and the arm will fall to your side again as you place your foot.

Figure 4

Now, you place your weight onto the left foot as you breathe in again and return your tongue to the upper palate. You will now bring your right or rear leg over the

Figure 5

Figure 6

fence as well. Open your right hip as you do this and look back slightly, as in Figure 5.

I sometimes call this posture "golden dog pisseth." Your rear leg comes all the way over the fence as your hips turn to the front, and as you breathe out, your tongue again goes to the bottom palate and you kick your right foot slowly in front of you, as in Figure 6.

You have now changed "posts." Your left leg is now the post, and only the right leg is moving, with the rest of the body totally balanced and relaxed on that one leg. Round your shoulders and hollow the chest as you do this.

Now, without losing the post, take that same (right) leg back up and over the fence as you inhale again, placing the tongue back onto the upper palate. Then as you kick the leg backward, as in Figure 7, you place your tongue back down onto the lower palate and breathe out.

Remember that there is a fence between your legs at this stage, so you cannot simply swing your leg backward. You must lift it back over the fence.

Again, as you lift your right leg back over the fence you breathe in and place your tongue back up, and you kick forward as before while you lower your tongue and breathe out. So you have lifted your right leg over the fence twice forward and once backward at this stage.

Figure 7

Now, as in Figure 8, place your right foot onto the ground and slowly shift your weight to it, so that your right leg again becomes the post.

Lift your left leg as you breathe in and move your tongue upward, only this time do not actually lift your leg over the fence, as it is now behind you. You now swing your left leg through to kick in

Figure 8

Figure 9

Figure 10

front of you as per a normal knee kick as you breathe out and lower your tongue (fig. 9).

Now swing your left foot back again while breathing in with the tongue on the upper palate, and as you kick back to the rear, lower your tongue and breathe out (fig. 10).

See how there is no appreciable lean on the back. It is kept as vertical as possible, keeping the right leg as the post. You do not look behind now.

As shown in Figure 11, swing your left leg to the front again, breathing in with tongue up, and as you kick forward, breathe out with tongue down.

You hold this posture, breathing naturally, not moving the tongue for a few seconds and then lower your left foot to the ground. You now begin the whole thing again, starting with the right foot forward.

Once you become used to this, you will be able to increase the speed slightly and you might even want to actually place an object about 30 inches high in front of you and step over it. Once you have the internal idea of the post, you will want to do this exercise quite often, as it is quite relaxing and calms the *shen* (spirit). After going through this exercise once or twice per day for one week, you will begin to feel the post rooting you to the ground, and you will feel more power in everything you do. You will now have tremendous power in

Figure 11

your punches without using the power of your legs to push forward, but rather using the power of the ground, which is enhanced by the waist. This is the true meaning of the classic saying from the old Chinese texts, "The power comes from the tan-tien to the bubbling spring (Kidney 1, or K 1, located in the depression between the mounts of the big toe and second toe), is directed through the legs and is controlled by the waist, which manifests in the fingers." In other words, we do not use the legs to push forward using physical power, but rather we use the post, which seems to suck us to the ground, allowing some "other" power to be directed to where it has to go for any particular work, without hindrance.

In another Chinese saying, the phrase "to know when there will be internal stillness" means that you will know when the post is working for you, as you will, for the first time, feel that stillness from within. It is like no other peace. It's inexplicable, so I will not even try.

The Third Post Exercise: The Bagwa Walking Post

This exercise provides all that is required for self-defense in the mind and body. It is easy, however, to do this exercise the wrong way, so pay great attention to what is being given here, particularly the correct placement of the feet. Later, I will give you things to do with your hands, as well as things to do with a partner in this exercise. But it is most important to focus on what your feet are doing first, as opposed to the hands.

In this exercise the footwork is primary, as we are learning the post. The hands are only there to enhance what we are doing with the feet.

Begin with the same stance as for the previous post exercise, with the left foot forward. Pick up your left foot. Notice that at first your whole body will move and cause the foot to lift up. This is wrong. When you pick up your left or front foot, you must not have any weight placed upon it to begin with. You will now be able to simply pick up that foot and move only the left leg. Nothing else

moves. You are as still as a mountain. Watch your arms in particular; be sure that they do not become tense. Just allow the arms to hang by your sides. If the left leg interferes with the left arm, just let that arm be pushed out of the way. Do not use any strength to move your arm out of the way. See Figure 12.

Once you are able to do this without moving any other part of your body, you should take your left

Figure 12

foot back to the rear behind your right foot, again without moving any part of your body except your left foot. Here's the important bit: place the left foot down behind the right foot with both the heel and the toes touching at precisely the same time, as shown in Figures 13 and 14.

Figure 13

You will feel some tension in your left leg and hip as you do this. Do not place the toes down before the heel; this is easy, and it is not

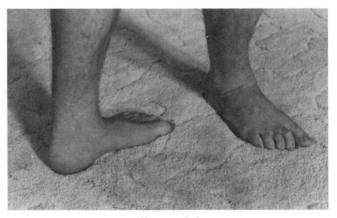

Figure 14

the post. You must stretch your left leg so that the heel touches the ground at the same time as the toes.

There is no special breathing with this exercise, other than normal, deep, natural breathing. Do not allow the

Figure 15

breath to rise into the upper chest; keep it low into the abdomen. As you breathe in, the abdomen expands; as you breathe out, it is contracted. In qigong breathing, this is called a "natural breath." Breathe in and out through the nose while doing this exercise slowly. You are learning qigong now, so the breathing is important. Later it will become quite fast and the breathing will not be as important,

Figure 16

as you will be learning about the martial application then. Do not speed it up yet, however, as you will lose the post and it will just become a stepping exercise instead of a post exercise.

25

You should now place your weight onto the left foot. Prior to this, there was absolutely no weight on that foot; it was just touching the ground. Now that you are weighted on the left foot, it becomes the post. Your right foot now scrapes past your left foot, moving parallel to it. (See figs. 15 and 16.)

Next, as shown in Figure 17, you take that right foot right back past the left foot, keeping it parallel to the left foot.

Figure 17

Now, the right foot does an arc back around to the front, still parallel to the left foot so that the toes are now leading, as in a hook kick (fig. 18).

This is your second step with no weight on the right foot. Remember, the toe and heel both leave and touch the ground at the same time.

You still have the post on the left foot as you take the third

Figure 18

Figure 19

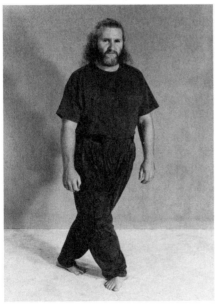

Figure 20

step. Your right foot steps across your left foot so that the front of the left knee and the back of the right knee are touching, with the heel and toe touching the ground simultaneously (fig. 19).

This was your third step. The fourth step is the hardest, physically, to do. You have to place your weight onto the right foot now, as in Figure 20.

Here comes the hard bit. You now have to pick up your left foot, heel, and toe together! Do not lift your heel up first. To do this, you should lift your right hip, which in turn picks up your left foot (fig. 21).

However, if I were to hold it as it is in the photo, this would be wrong. In the previous posture, I built up potential energy in my waist in the form of a twisting of the body. When I lift the left foot, that twist will release and my left foot will swing back to the front again in an arc, as in the beginning stance. (See fig. 22.)

Again your left foot has done an arc with no weight on it. You are now back into a right-post stance. You have to switch to the other side, and the stepping gives us a way of doing so without just stopping and starting again. The above is one completed round of post stepping, beginning on the right with the left foot forward and finishing with the left foot forward.

The two steps to get to the beginning of the other side are as follows. From the beginning (ending) stance (fig. 22), rather than performing the whole thing again on that side as you normally would, take a step with your left foot across the front of your right foot (fig. 23).

Next, you perform the more difficult step that you did earlier, only in reverse. Your right foot now has to

Figure 21

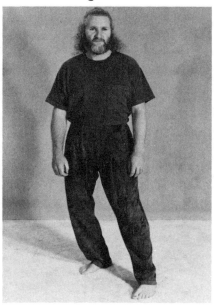

Figure 22

Figure 23

Figure 24

come off the ground, heel and toe together (fig. 24). Again swing around to the front so it ends up forward. (fig. 25).

You are now in exactly the opposite position of that which you were in to begin with. So you have taken two steps to get you to the other side. Now you can perform the whole four steps in reverse, beginning by taking your right foot behind your left foot, as in Figure 26, then sliding your left foot past your right foot and arcing it around to the front, as in Figure 27.

Now take the left foot across the right foot (fig. 28), finishing up by again lifting the right foot off the ground, heel and toe together, and swinging it around to the front to end up as you started.

You do this stepping on the left side a few times and then reverse it back to the original side by taking the right foot across the left foot to get back to the beginning again. So, after you have done the four steps on one side a few times, you change direction by stepping across the front instead of taking the front foot behind.

A Dim-Mak Technique to Remember the Footwork

I always tell my students when trying to learn the dim-mak points or techniques that it is best to learn anything with some particular reference to yourself, and not by writing on your arms in black ink. Then it just becomes a whole lot of numbers or points. It is also better to learn individual points in acupuncture by coupling them to something that has particular reference to yourself, rather than learning all of them parrot fashion.

So here we have a multiple dim-mak

Figure 25

Figure 26

Figure 27

Figure 28

technique, one that you would probably never use, as it is just too complicated for street defense. However, if you can sort of get this multitechnique with a level of competence, then you will find that the simpler ones come more easily. Also, each individual technique within this multitechnique can be taken by itself and used to great advantage.

You have a partner attack with a left jab. You are standing with your left foot forward as in the beginning of the post. As he comes in, you take that first step with your left foot behind your right foot, exactly as you did in the second post exercise. Remember to place the foot with heel and toe together. As you do this, you slam his left arm at the elbow to a point called Colon 12 (Co 12), just above the elbow on the outside of the arm (fig. 29).

Your right palm

continues down his arm to end up at his wrist as your right fingers strike to the side of his neck at Stomach 9 (St 9), the carotid point (fig. 30), located in the depression underneath the jaw, just left and slightly above his Adam's apple.

Your weight is now on your left leg. As you take your next step with your right foot, scraping it by your left foot, your palms change over. The left one hammers to the Heart 5 (H 5) and Lung 8 (Lu 8) points just above the wrist crease, toward his elbow. You do not actually pull his wrist, but rather, you strike both sides of his wrist using your fingers in a grabbing motion with a fa-jing shake. (Fa-jing, which I covered in *Dim-Mak: Death-Point Striking* and also in great detail in my video numbered MTG34, means "explosive energy," and is manifested

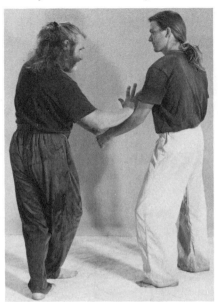

Figure 29

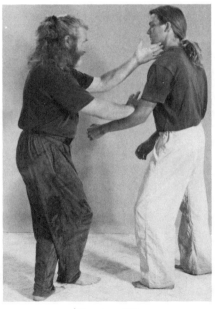

Figure 30

Figure 31

Figure 32

when the whole body explodes into action, a little like sneezing while punching.)

If your partner is not shook up from this and only pulled forward, then you are not doing it correctly. It should be just the same body movement as a punch, but in reverse.

A split second later, the fingers of the right palm attack to his Governor Vessel (Gv 26) point, just under the nose, as in Figure 31.

As anyone who has been lightly struck at Gv 26 knows, a harder strike and you're in trouble. Combine it with the draining effect of H 5 and Lu 8, and you have a death-point strike. But we are not finished yet. Remember that your right foot still has to swing around. It does this a split second after the last two strikes, striking into Kidney 10 (K 10), just in back of his knee (fig. 32).

If he has taken a reverse stance to attack

33

you initially, then you should attack to Spleen 10 (Sp 10), on the inside of his thigh, just up from the knee, as in Figure 33. (This is a controlling point, which is covered in Chapter 6.)

Figure 33

So you have now performed the first two steps from the bagwa walking post that we did solo earlier, only you've added some pretty deadly dim-mak point strikes. You still have the last two steps to perform. Your attacker, to allow you to learn the steps, attacks with his right fist to your head. With the back of your right palm, you attack to a nerve point on the inside of his elbow (fig. 34).

Now this strike is not at all tense; in fact, it is called a "dead arm." The arm is totally relaxed, and only the body gives it movement—yet it is about three times as hard as a tense arm. Again, do not do this for real with your training partners, as you will run out of

Figure 34

Figure 35

Figure 36

them very soon! The nerves we strike at here to take out the arm are the musculo-cutaneous nerve and the radialis nerve. (I'll explain the difference between nerve strikes and dim-mak strikes in Chapter 3.) Your right foot steps across as you do this strike, as shown in Figure 34. This is your third step.

You now twist your body so that your right palm is able to move his right arm across to your right as you change the post to your left foot, as in Figure 35.

Your right palm now moves on top of his right wrist and takes control of it. Now, as you lift your left foot, heel, and toe together, using that natural swing of your body to move your left arm around, you slam him in the back of the head at a point called Gall Bladder 19 (Gb 19). As shown in Figure 36, your left foot comes around again to the front as this happens. (For the precise location of Gb 19, refer to Figure 199 in Chapter 6.)

As this happens, you should shock his heart and lungs again by negatively striking to the wrist points, as described above, just before you strike up and over his head with your left palm to Gb 19. To positively charge the palm before the strike, hold it so that the wrist is bent downward (limp). The palm is now said to be full of yang energy. As you strike to Gb 19, the palm is flexed backward, thus releasing the yang energy into the point. This is a knockout point and is quite sensitive, as many important cranial nerves are located near it. With the use of the set-up points (see *Dim-Mak: Death-Point Striking*) on the wrist, Lung 9 and Heart 5, some people will go into knockout with only the lightest touch to Gb 19. Others need a little more power. When practicing this technique, always keep clear of the real points, as the ones at the back of the head are really dangerous.

You can practice the above technique on the other side, of course. But be sure that you do not lose sight of the fact that the primary goal is gaining the post, and not the actual technique. We only practice this technique to learn the stepping correctly.

A Dim-Mak Technique to Remember the Footwork

All of the above has been a sort of abstract way of learning about the movement of the legs and feet for dim-mak. Now we have an abstract way of learning about the hands

Figure 37

Figure 38

Figure 39

and arms for dim-mak. For this exercise we use the same stepping pattern just covered, only now, the arms begin to move with the steps.

If you hold your arms as in Figure 37, this is representative in an abstract way of everything we do with the arms in the martial arts. Notice how the elbows are held so that there is some distance at your axilla. The space this position creates under your arms is called the *kua* (or "bridge"). The palms are not held rigid but relaxed; the whole arm is hanging off of the shoulders. The elbows are held upward but not so high as to raise them above the shoulders. One hand is held a little forward of the inside of the other elbow (in this case it is the left hand that is held a little forward). In this solo exercise, all you are going to do with your arms is reverse the positions of both hands when you take your first and last steps in the bagwa walking post routine.

A change of hands in bagwa is as follows. Bring the right hand under the left wrist, touching, as in Figure 38. Then continue sliding it forward until you end up in the opposite position (fig. 39). This is all the hands and arms will do. So as you take your first step back with your left foot, your right palm comes under your left so that by the time the weight has gone onto the left foot, the hands are held as in Figure 40.

You should hold this hand position for the next step with your right foot, arcing it back to the rear and bringing it forward in exactly the same way as you learned before. But now, as your right foot has made contact with the ground, there is a slight shake of your body that will reach your palms and cause

Figure 40

Figure 41

Figure 42

Figure 43

them to shake. The wrists must be so relaxed that they actually vibrate as this happens. I have tried to show this in the following photos. Figure 41 shows the body moving slightly forward to begin the shake, and there has been a slight turning of the waist to the left which causes the right arm to move outward and the left palm to move backward. Now, as the weight sits fully back again, the waist turns slightly to your right, causing your right palm to move back and your left palm to move forward (fig. 42). Again the waist moves back to the left to the starting position, thus bringing your palms back to normal again (fig. 43).

If this happens quickly, the movement is barely visible to the observer, but you will know that it has happened internally; only your wrists will vibrate. This is how we begin to learn about how to use internal strength—we learn how to "put the qi into the points" using this method.

You are now ready to take your third step. Remember that the hands only change on the first and last steps, so here the hands do not change. You simply take the third step with your right foot across your left knee while holding your arms the same way (fig. 44). As you begin to take your final step with the left foot, you should do the change moving your left palm under your right wrist, as in Figure 45. Finish up as in Figure 46, the same way that you began. You must also repeat the vibration of the palms as you just did, only in reverse, to finish.

When you change the direction of the stepping by stepping across in front, the arms stay the same for the first step across but

Figure 44

Figure 45

Figure 46

Figure 47

change for the second step and vibrate upon completion. Then you can perform the whole thing on the opposite side, starting with the right foot and hand forward.

Using a Partner

I would suggest that you master the above before going on to the next phase of this post training. This is where we use a force on our arms to get the feeling of "putting in the qi." This is a most important part of learning about internal power and the gaining of it.

Your partner is only there to assist you, not to be in competition with you. He or she will only be applying a constant force onto your arms as you walk. This will give you an idea of how your post is coming along and how your hands are learning the idea of "putting in."

You begin as in Figure 47, with the left foot forward. Your partner is placing his hands onto your left forearm and wrist, applying just enough pressure so that he does not push you over and so that you do not have to lean forward onto him to avoid falling backward. This is very important, and if your partner feels that you are leaning upon him, he should pull away quickly to show you that you are. If you are holding your back in the "C" position, it should not be too difficult to maintain an upward posture without leaning forward.

Figure 48

You take his weight on your left arm and begin your first step, standing as still as a mountain as your left foot comes off the ground. As you do this, your right arm will come underneath as before to "take over" the pressure (fig. 48). You hold his pressure as you place your weight onto your left foot (fig. 49). Now, you hold his pressure with your right arm as you take your second step

Figure 49

Figure 50

Figure 51

with your right foot (fig. 50).

Here, the shake should send a slight shock wave into his body as you do it. It is important to not have the power moving to your left side, thus simply pushing his arms over to your left. Nor should you be trying to push him backward, as this is only a push. You should be trying to send a small shock wave into his center using your waist and arms, finishing up at your palms. The movement is so small that it cannot actually push him backward, so if you are doing so, it's wrong. There is no way to take a photo of this, so you will just have to work on it.

You should now take your third step, still holding his pressure on your right arm so that your right foot is again across your left (fig. 51). The next step is the most difficult, as you must stop yourself from falling backward.

As you change your weight to your right foot, your left palm comes underneath your right wrist, ready for the takeover of his pressure (fig. 52). You pick up your left foot and, taking over his pressure with your left palm, take your final step (fig. 53). You again send a shock wave into his center by the use of your waist and arms.

You cannot learn about internal power by using objects to train with. There is an old Chinese saying that comes from Yang Lu-ch'an's response to the question of whether there were any men he could not beat using internal power. "Yes," he replied. "Men of stone, men of iron, and men of wood." What he meant is that you cannot use dim-mak—*real* dim-mak—against pieces of wood and other inanimate objects. So people who say that they are using internal methods to break boards and stones, etc.,

Figure 52

Figure 53

are up themselves (i.e., "not being truthful to themselves," "kidding themselves"), to use a good Oz colloquialism! When we train, we must train with people. This is the *only* way to learn about applying dim-mak at a high level of internal energy and not just at a physical level of "hit the point and knock him out!"

The above is the best method I know of for learning about your own body-mind coordination and the gaining of the internal power necessary for dim-mak. It is also the best exercise for learning balance and timing on a physical level. We also learn subconsciously about never using a human technique when we are attacked, but rather reacting instantly and without human remorse or feeling. This is the way of the reptile.

The Original Dim-Mak Point Techniques

2

I n this chapter, I will show a short but important kata or form that will teach you about the original dim-mak strikes. When the taiji form was first invented, it was not as long as it is today. However, hidden within this short form were the most deadly strikes known.

I will give one complete movement of the form or kata, followed by the application.

The Form: Move No. 1

Stand with your feet parallel, shoulder width apart, your arms relaxed by your sides. Place your tongue onto your hard palate and breathe slowly and deeply without raising the chest as you breathe in. Your shoulders should be relaxed and hanging naturally rounded, and the chest should be relaxed and slightly concave. This is standing as we normally should as human beings, without tension (fig. 54).

Each palm will do a counterclockwise circle—out to your right, over to your left, and back down to the starting position. The left palm should lead the right palm; they should not move simultaneously. As you do this, you will shift your weight slightly to the right foot, then forward onto the ball of your right foot, then over to the ball of your left foot, and finally back onto your heels. As this weight change occurs, you turn your waist slightly to the right and then, as your hands come back down, turn to the left and back to the front. Your whole body has done a counterclockwise circle. This has happened because of the weight changes and the turning of the waist. (See figs. 55, 56, 57, and 58.) Note how the palms "cut" upward with their outside edges.

Figure 54

Figure 55

Figure 56

Figure 57

Figure 58

Technique No. 1

Your opponent attacks with a right straight to your head. You move your body (the first weight change) to get out of the way as your left palm attacks to Neigwan (Pericardium 6, or Pc 6) on the inside of his forearm (fig. 59). You have just moved within range of his left fist. You block this also into Neigwan, using your right palm (fig. 60).

You now go on the attack. Your left palm slams downward into

Figure 59

Figure 60

Figure 61

Stomach 15 and Stomach 16 on his right pectoral. This will affect the heart, especially since you have set up these points by striking to Neigwan (fig. 61). Your right palm (which is following your left) now also strikes downward into St 15 and St 16 on his left pectoral (fig. 62).

You practice this with your attacker throwing his first two punches as quickly as he can. You must do the movement as quickly as you can without losing the technique. Your partner then determines whether or not to put in the second attack. You do not wait, however, but continue with your own attack regardless of what he does. So sometimes you will be blocking his second attack, while sometimes you will just carry on as if you *have* blocked his second attack.

This is the training method for gaining awareness and not allowing the attacker to

51

cause you to do what he wants you to do.

The Form: Move No. 2

Moving on from the first movement (fig. 58), your palms swing out to your right side with the left one leading. Your weight has again changed to your right foot and your waist has turned to your right (fig. 63). Your palms continue up and over to your left, and the weight moves accordingly so that, as you move into the position shown in Figure 64, the weight comes forward onto the balls of the feet. Your body is again doing a counterclockwise circle and, at this point, has come halfway around.

Figure 62

Figure 63

Figure 64

Technique No. 2

He attacks with a left straight. You shift your weight to evade as both your palms swing out to your right, your left palm taking his left forearm over to your left (blocking) as your right fingers attack to Gall Bladder 1 (Gb 1), a knockout point, at the outer corner of his eye (fig. 65).

Figure 65

The Form: Move No. 3

Continuing from Figure 64, you now change your weight to your left foot, as your left palm begins to change to a flexed (yang) hand and your right palm has changed to a limp (yin) palm (fig. 66). Continuing, your left palm moves down in an arc to your left. As your weight changes to your right foot, that foot turns 45 degrees to your right. Your left palm has come across to your right and has now gone limp (yin), as your right palm has become yang (fig. 67).

Technique No. 3

He now attacks with a right rip to your left rib area. Your left palm moves down as your weight changes to your left foot. Your left palm now bumps his right forearm over to your right, thus blocking. As this happens, your right fingers attack to his eyes (fig. 68). You have also

Figure 66

Figure 67

Figure 68

Figure 69

changed your weight to your right foot, thus pulling his arm further over to your right.

The Form: Move No. 4

Continuing from the attack to his eyes (fig. 67), your waist—not your hips—moves to your right slightly as your left palm flexes and pushes out to the front. (The waist is that which is above the sacrum, or upper pelvic structure, while the hip is that which is below the sacrum, including the sacrum. The hips and waist can move independently of each other.) Your right fingers now go yin (fig. 69).

Technique No. 4

After you have defeated his right rip (fig. 68), you further attack, this time to the girdle meridian. This is the "extra" meridian that runs around the waist, just over the hip-bone (fig. 70). You attack this meridian just over the top and

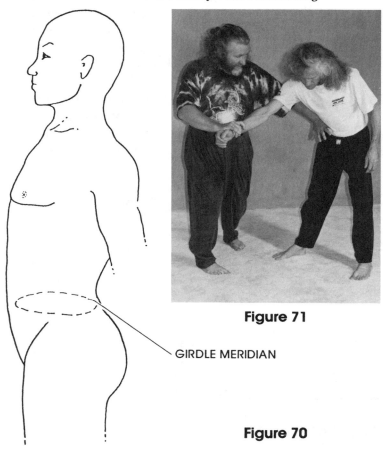

Figure 71

GIRDLE MERIDIAN

Figure 70

down into the hipbone (fig. 71). This has the effect of causing his upper body to be "disconnected" (internally, in terms of energy) from his lower body and making him totally scattered mentally.

In striking the girdle meridian at this point, you are also striking to Gall Bladder 28 (Gb 28), which is a knockout point located just under the highest part of the hip, about 2 inches below the navel. Notice that your right palm has struck his right wrist area (down his arm toward his fingers, "hammering" onto the bones of his wrist), thus activating H 5 and L 8 points on the inside of his wrist. Heart 5 and Lung 8 in par-

Figure 72

Figure 73

ticular are energy drainage points for the heart and the seat of power (the lungs).

The Form: Move No. 5

From Form Move No. 4 (fig. 69), you should take a left step forward (fig. 72). As you bring your weight forward to that foot, your left palm moves upward as your right palm moves downward. Your waist turns to the front (fig. 73).

Technique No. 5

You step forward to "close" (move toward him). Your right palm again pulls violently downward on his right wrist, thus compressing his ribs. Your left palm attacks upward under his arm to Heart 1 (H 1), directly into his armpit (fig. 74). This stops his heart from beating and brings us to the end of one section of movement where the techniques are concerned.

Figure 74

In all of the above we have been defending and attacking the same attacker, with all of the techniques leading up to stopping the heart, although any one of the techniques alone would stop him.

The Form: Move No. 6

From the position shown in Figure 73, your right palm goes yin as your left palm goes yang and your waist turns slightly to your left (fig. 75). Your waist now turns slightly to your right as both

Figure 75

Figure 76

Figure 77

palms change state (fig. 76).

Technique No. 6

Someone attacks with a right hook to your ribs again. This time, you will be blocking on his "open" side. When you block his right arm (on the outside of it), you are standing on the "closed" side. You are in no danger of his other hand, as you are standing on his right side. If you block that same arm on the open side (the inside of his arm), you are in danger of his other hand (as you are now standing in front of him).

Your right palm bumps the inside of his right forearm as your left palm slams down on top of it, thus blocking and striking to two points. These need not be specific points, as slamming down in this way will strike to heart and lung points on the ulna, or little-finger side, of his forearm and to the radius side,

59

respectively (fig. 77). This is energy draining. Your right palm now attacks to his girdle meridian as your left palm jerks his right wrist violently downward (fig. 78).

The Form: Move No. 7

From the position shown in Figure 76, your right foot lifts up and steps to your right. It lands in the same place it came from, only it is now pointing to your right. As you bring your weight onto that foot, your right palm will change state (go to yin) as your left palm goes to yang, and both palms move forward and upward (fig. 79).

Technique No. 7

From the position in Figure 78, you step to "close" with your right foot. As you bring your weight forward, your right palm attacks to his neck area (St 9), while your left palm "scrapes" up the inside of his arm vio-

Figure 78

Figure 79

Figure 80

Figure 81

lently and ends up striking to Spleen 19 (Sp 19), which is just upward from the crease of his axilla and on the front of his shoulder (fig. 80). This combination of points not only causes a knockout (St 9), but also causes his legs to give way (Sp 19).

The Form: Move No. 8
You turn both palms over where they are as you move your waist slightly to your right, so that your palms end up over the top of your right knee, as in Figure 81. As you sit back onto your left foot, your palms drop down and change state. Your hips and waist have turned to your left, thus giving the effect of the palms being pulled to your left. Actually, they have only moved downward. It is the body moving that gives the impression that the arms are moving to the side (fig. 82). Notice that the palms

have changed state so that the left palm is now yin and the right one is yang. You lift your left palm and join it to the inside of your right wrist (fig. 83). The state of the palms has not changed. Now you lift both palms up to chest height as you change your weight to your right foot and turn your hips to the front. Both palms change state, thus providing great power for this strike (fig. 84).

Figure 82

Figure 83

Figure 84

Figure 85

Technique No. 8

He attacks with a right rip to your lower left rib area. Both your palms turn over and cut across his neck, with your right palm striking to St 9 and your left to Small Intestine 16 (Si 16), in the middle of the side of the neck where it makes contact with the shoulders (fig. 85). Now, slam down onto the inside of the crease of his forearm (using your right palm) and also onto Neigwan with your left palm (fig. 86). The nerve strike gives him a dead arm, while the Neigwan strike sets up the next strike and causes him to feel really ill.

Figure 86

Without stopping, you now join your left wrist to the inside of your right wrist and, coming forward, attack to Liver 14 (Liv 14) with the back of your right wrist (fig. 87). Liv 14, located 1.5 cun (about 1.5 inches) below the nipple where the pectorals make a crease, is a death point, and it is extremely sensitive. (*Cun* is a measurement used in traditional Chinese medicine. It varies from person to person but is generally about the length from the first knuckle of your index finger to the second—about an inch.)

This completes this section of techniques, all of which were aimed at the final strike to Liv 14. The next lot of techniques begins with a new attacker.

Figure 87

Figure 88

Figure 89

The Form: Move No. 9

From the position shown in Figure 84, your body moves backward slightly as both palms change state and your hips turn to your left (fig. 88). You now turn your body back to the front slightly, as you move your weight back onto your right foot fully. Your palms again change state (fig. 89). Both palms have done a counterclockwise circle.

Again your palms change state and your body moves backward, turning to the left (fig. 90). As your body turns to the front, you join your left palm to the inside of your right wrist, without the palms changing the state (fig. 91). Now you bring your weight forward and drop both palms downward as they change state, thus attacking (fig. 92).

Figure 90

Figure 91

Figure 92

Figure 93

Technique No. 9

Suppose someone attacks you with a right straight to your head. You sit back slightly, turning to your left as your left palm attacks to his Neigwan point. Your right palm attacks to Heart 3 (H 3) point at his elbow crease, thus upsetting his heartbeat (fig. 93). You continue upsetting his heart by attacking with your right palm to St 9 as your left palm scrapes up the inside of his right fore-arm, thus setting up the point (fig. 94).

You again sit back and grab his right wrist with your left palm and again attack to H 3 (fig. 95). Now, you turn to him and move your weight forward as both of your palms slam downward into Liv 14 (fig. 96). This strike will drain so much energy from his lungs that he will either die or be unable to continue (but he does in this case, just for the exercise).

Figure 94

Figure 95

Figure 96

Figure 97

The Form: Move No. 10

From the position shown in Figure 92, slide your palms apart as you begin to sit back onto your left leg and turn your hips to your left. Sit back so that you have 70 percent of your weight on your left leg and 30 percent on your right. Your palms should open up so that they end up over the top of their respective knees (fig. 97).

As you begin to turn your hips back to

the front, you should scoop your right palm so that the fingers poke forward in a jabbing motion. At the same time, the palm of the left hand also begins to scoop and poke (fig. 98). Finish off this posture as you sit fully onto your left leg by now poking with the fingers of your left palm. Note that the right fingers poke first, followed by the left fingers (fig. 99).

Continuing, begin bringing your weight forward. As you do this, lift your right elbow upward in a strike as your hips turn your torso to your left slightly (fig. 100). Now, as you continue bringing your weight forward, turn your hips to your right and bring your left elbow upward in a strike (fig. 101). As you finish bringing your weight forward, turn your hips slightly to your left again and claw downward with the fingers of your right

Figure 98

Figure 99

Figure 100

palm (fig. 102). As you place 70 percent of your weight onto your right foot, turn your hips back to the front and claw downward with your left fingers (fig. 103).

Figure 101

Figure 102

Figure 103

Figure 104

Figure 105

Technique No. 10

Your attacker/partner tries to strike to your lower right rib area with a left hook. You should sit back and slam the inside of his left forearm at Neigwan with your right heel-palm. This alone will cause him to feel ill so that he has to sit down (fig. 104). Taiji is the art of overkill, so you should now attack to Liver 13 with the fingers of your right palm, as in Figure 105. (Liv 13 is located at the tip of the free rib and the eleventh rib.) This will cause a knockout because of the point's association with the gall-bladder meridian and with Liv 14. It will also cause major psychological disorders later in life! Liv 13 is over the top of major internal organs, so striking this point also does gross internal physical damage.

Your left fingers now attack to his opposite Liv 13 point (fig. 106). You have struck to both Liv 13 points, but not simultaneously. (No two points are struck simultaneously in dim-mak; there is a slight delay between strikes, sometimes only a split second.)

Now, as you begin to close on him, your right elbow attacks to Gb 24 on his left side, about 2 inches below the nipple and verticle to it, just below Liv 14 (fig. 107). This will cause a knockout at least, and death at the most. Without stopping, your left elbow now attacks to Gb 24 point on his right side (fig. 108). You continue the attack, this time with your right fingers to his eyes, gouging downward into the sockets (fig. 109). Your left "claw" now attacks to his clavicle (collarbone) at the Stomach 11 and 12 (St 11 and St 12) points, located just above the collarbone notch where it is closest to the neck. The strike to St 11 causes his vagus nerve to act upon the

Figure 106

Figure 107

Figure 108

Figure 109

cardio-inhibitory center in the brain, causing a knockout. Striking St 12 by clawing down into the collarbone will take his will to fight away (fig. 110).

Generations of genius have added to the original dim-mak techniques, until today we have quite a long form. In fact, it is probably the longest form of any martial art, with each of the 300-some postures having its own dim-mak application. This is what makes this art of taiji the most deadly ever invented.

All of the modern martial art styles of today owe their dim-mak applications to the original style of taiji. It's unfortunate that dim-mak lives on primarily in these contemporary "hard styles," and not in the original style, due mainly to the somewhat mystical name that taiji has gained over the years. However, I am trying to rectify this.

At the time of this

writing, I am working on a book that will show all of the 300 or so movements and their dim-mak applications.

My video series *Taiji to the Max* shows the whole original Yang Lu-ch'an-style taiji form at its most advanced level and gives each posture's deadly dim-mak applications.

Figure 110

Nerves or Points

3

Nerve strikes are aimed at specific nerve targets on the body. In striking to nerves, we upset the nervous system, sometimes causing the whole body to shut down and go into knockout. At a lesser level, we can strike to nerves to cause, for instance, an arm to go dead or a leg to become weak so that the person being struck falls down.

Strikes to dim-mak points, on the other hand, affect the internal organs of the body and not necessarily the nervous system. This type of strike will also cause knockout and, at its most dangerous, death. Using the dim-mak points, we can cause the body we are striking to do what we want it to do (i.e., fall down, go into knockout, etc.). We can also cause energy drainage from the body, thus also bringing about a knockout or death. Conversely, we can use these same points to heal the damage we have done, whereas when we strike to nerves, we are not able to use those same points to heal the damage.

Nerve strikes cause great pain, while dim-mak strikes cause internal reactions to take place and do not necessarily cause pain. Dim-mak points mostly rely upon human phenomena to gain their effect, as in the case of the carotid sinus or the neurological shutdown strikes (see *Dim-Mak: Death-Point Striking* for further detail).

Many people who study dim-mak, and any type of point striking (point striking is also called "cavity striking," "nerve striking," or "pressure-point striking"), are confused as to exactly what it is their teachers are telling them to strike: is it a nerve strike or is it a dim-mak strike? The confusion has come about as a result of teachers teaching both types of strikes, not knowing themselves exactly what it is they are striking to and what the difference is.

There *is* a difference between nerve point strikes and dim-mak point strikes. However, in many instances, one can strike both nerve and dim-mak points at the same time. This is because there are important nerve points that lie right under dim-mak points, and there are important dim-mak points where nerve points are located. Sometimes it is the nerve that reacts when you strike a dim-mak point, while often it is the dim-mak point that reacts when you are aiming for a nerve point (same location, different effect). You can strike to the dim-mak point Stomach 9, the carotid sinus, and at the same time cause nerve damage by attacking the vagus nerve, which runs alongside the internal carotid artery. The internal carotid artery is a branch of the main carotid artery that runs up under the sternocleidomastoid muscle from the base of the neck into the head and face. This artery houses the carotid sinus, the baroreceptor whose job it is to control the blood pressure in the body by its action upon the cardio-inhibitory center in the brain, which in turn controls the heart rate. In fact, it is very hard not to strike this nerve when aiming for the St 9 point. For the most part, though, nerve strikes and dim-mak strikes are separate. Chapter 6 will discuss the different ways to cause knockout effectively using either nerve or dim-mak strikes.

Figure 111

Figure 112

SAME LOCATION, SAME EFFECT

When we strike to St 9, we can affect the heart by causing the carotid sinus to act. Things inside the carotid sinus called pressoreceptors send signals to the cardio-inhibitory center via the vagus nerve to tell the heart to slow down or even stop beating. If, however, we strike the vagus nerve and not the carotid sinus, this will also signal the heart to slow down. So, in this case, either strike will have the same effect upon the heart and cause a knockout.

Femoral Nerve and Siqiang

The dim-mak point called siqiang (one of the "new points," discovered after the traditional points were documented, which are not necessarily on any meridian) is situated 4.5 cun (about 4.5 inches) above the midpoint of the superior border of the patella, or kneecap. This is a typical case where either a dim-mak point or a nerve point can be struck to great effect. Both have almost the same effect—paralysis of the leg, which causes the person to have to sit down.

This point can be struck with a heel, as in Figure 111, or with a palm, as in Figure 112. For the dim-mak point, however, it must always be struck in an upward way to cause qi drainage. This gives the feeling of extreme

Figure 113

fatigue. We cannot strike this point without also striking the femoral nerve (see fig. 111). To gain the most from this nerve strike, we must strike straight inward at a 180-degree angle to the thigh (fig. 113). The beauty of this strike is that you do not have to be pinpoint-accurate, as you will damage the femoral nerve even if you miss the dim-mak point of siqiang (refer to fig. 115).

The point called siqiang is situated right over the femoral nerve, and the needling of this point is probably associated with the nerve in that it affects the nerve. Many of the dim-mak points have no particular organ or nerve situated directly below them, but there are also many that do, and Western medical terms can be used to explain their effectiveness either in the dim-mak area or the acupuncture area.

The same cannot be said for all of the points where both dim-mak and nerve points lie together. Sometimes, depending upon the point and the way in which it is struck, the dim-mak points and the nerve points bring about totally different effects.

Same Location, Different Effects
Median Nerve and Heart 3

For instance, we could strike to a nerve point in the crease of the elbow to the inside of the arm, as in Figure 114. This is the area where we are able to attack the "median

nerve" to cause great nervous damage, which will "take the arm out" or, if the strike is hard enough, cause the nervous system to send the body into spasm. If, however, we strike the dim-mak point called Heart 3, which is also in this area, this will cause the heart to falter and/or stop. Same location, but different effects.

Cutaneous Femoris Nerve and Gall Bladder 31

Figure 114

A branch of the external cutaneous femoris nerve runs down the outside of the thigh (see fig. 115).

This nerve, when attacked with, for instance, a kick, as in Figure 116, will cause the leg to go dead, and the person will fall down. However, there is a much more dangerous strike that we can use here, depending upon our accuracy in kicking. The dim-mak point called Gall Bladder 31 (Gb 31), which lies just below the longest finger on the outside of the thigh when the arm is allowed to hang naturally at one's side, will cause the knockout effect by the carotid sinus' action on the heart. (In my first book, I explained exactly why this happens when any of the gall bladder points are struck.) So, if we kick to this point using either the tip of our shoe or the ball of the foot, as in Figure 117, we will not only damage the nerve but also bring about the knockout that results when Gb 31 is struck. I had some people who liked to go into tournaments and they used this kick to great advantage. Prior to that, they were using the old low roundhouse kick to the thigh area. As we all know, sometimes this just does no damage other than to wear your opponent down, whereas the Gb 31 kick will down him on your first strike.

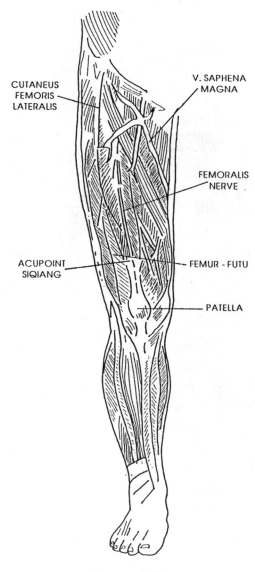

CUTANEUS FEMORIS LATERALIS

V. SAPHENA MAGNA

FEMORALIS NERVE

ACUPOINT SIQIANG

FEMUR - FUTU

PATELLA

Figure 115

We normally strike nerves that come close to the sur-

Figure 116

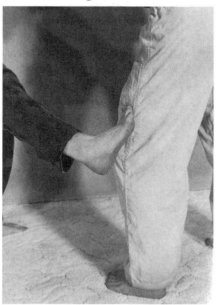

Figure 117

face of the body, as in the cases above, with the inside of the elbow and outside of the thigh. However, there are times when we can cause nerve damage from different types of attacks. The median nerve runs down on the inside of the fore-arm, midline. How-ever, this nerve is not as close to the outside of the arm as the other nerves I have dis-cussed in this chapter, and so we attack this nerve more toward the wrist area, where it is easier to get at.

We can attack this nerve with a strike (Figs. 118 and 119), using either the back of the palm or a penetra-tion punch as our opponent attacks us, for instance. Or we can use a lock (fig. 120) to attack all three major striking nerves in the forearm: the median, the ulnaris, and the radial, which will cause the whole arm to go into nervous spasm. (A "lock" is where we take a joint of the body and hold it in a way that places great pressure on that joint, causing pain. If the person moves, we increase the pressure to stop him from moving; thus, he is "locked.")

Figure 118

Figure 119

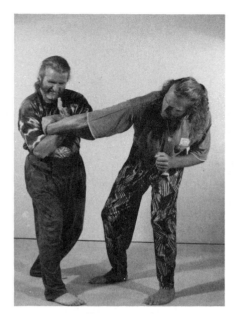

Figure 120

Medial, Ulnaris, and Radial Nerves
with Heart 4, 5, and 6 Plus Lung 8

We could use a lock from both taiji and bagwa. As the adversary attacks, we should use a damaging block to the radial and ulnaris nerves. As he attacks low, for instance, with a right hook to our lower left rib area, we should use our right forearm as the "hinge" and slam his arm, while slamming the topside of his arm with our left palm, as in Figure 121. (This is the only way that locks and holds will ever work; you must stun the attacker first so that you can get the lock on. Never try to get a lock on if the attacker is fully alert and in full yang state.)

This is the first attack, and it is to the radial and ulnaris nerves. It allows us to now slap the top of his right palm to cause his fist to relax and bend (fig. 122). Notice how I have placed my right palm, bending greatly around his wrist. Now, I should pull his right arm in toward my belly, causing it to further fold and to be trapped with my right palm and my belly (fig. 123). I am now able to simply turn

Figure 121

my waist to my right to cause great nerve damage and to control my opponent, leaving my left hand clear to attack any other points to take him out completely if I wish (fig. 124).

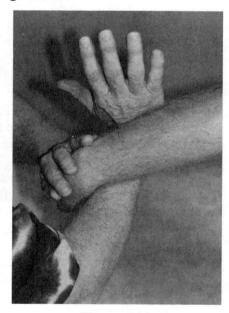

Figure 122

Figure 123

Figure 124

Figure 125

Figure 126

Figure 127

Figure 128

I also could attack to the median nerve on the inside middle of his forearm. As he attacks with a straight right, I could slam the inside of his arm with my right palm toward me (this is also a setup dim-mak strike) as my left palm is coming underneath my right (fig. 125). I am now free to slam him in the neck using the back of my right palm to the vagus nerve. This alone will knock him out (fig. 126). My left palm is still controlling his right arm. Now, my right palm grabs over the top of his right wrist, as in Figure 127, and my ring finger digs deeply into the inside of his forearm. I now turn my waist to my right, which causes my right fingers to dig in more to the median nerve. This he cannot resist and so goes down (fig. 128).

Heart 4, 5, and 6 plus Lung 8

The above nerve strikes were to nerves that are more inside of the forearm. However, I could have used those same techniques to strike to dim-mak points, wreaking far greater havoc than nervous damage alone. In the first instance, when I locked the wrist, I also attacked to Heart 4, 5, and 6 and Lung 8 (on the inside of the wrist, as shown in Figure 129). Together these are energy-draining points and will take away the attacker's will to carry on with the attack. I would further attack to heart and lung points as I took him down as in the previous photo (Fig. 128).

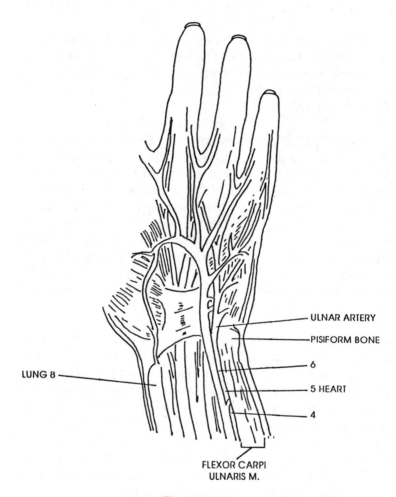

ULNAR ARTERY

PISIFORM BONE

6

5 HEART

4

LUNG 8

FLEXOR CARPI
ULNARIS M.

Figure 129

Pericardium 6
This technique is also used as a dim-mak strike to
Neigwan, or Pericardium 6 (Pc 6), located on the inside of
the wrist, three fingers' width back from the wrist crease
in the inside center of the forearm. All that is required to
attack to Neigwan is to have your ring finger in the correct
place on the inside of the forearm. This has an extreme

draining effect and allows you to control the attacker better than if you used the nerve strike only.

With the above strikes we cannot help but strike to nerves as well as dim-mak points if we know where the dim-mak points lie, but an effect will be produced even if we miss the dim-mak point, as the nerve points work very well by themselves.

Stomach 32 and the Femoral Nerve

Stomach 32 (St 32) is also in the vicinity of siqiang but is not placed over the femoral nerve, and striking this point produces a very definite dim-mak result, i.e., extreme nausea and energy drainage. St 32 is situated right over the top of the femur and so is a little right of center on the right leg and a little left of center on the left leg. If you place your wristband area on the upper border of the patella and then lay your palm down flat over the thigh, St 32 lies roughly where your longest finger ends (see fig. 129). This point is usually struck with a blunt instrument, like the heel-palm, for instance.

Liver 14 and the Lungs

The relationship between dim-mak points, nerve points, and normal physical trauma on the anterior of the trunk is complicated, as there are just so many dangerous points to strike in this area. One never really knows what is being struck. We could, for instance, strike to the dim-mak point called Liver 14, on the pectorals, in a straight line with Conceptor Vessel 14 (Cv 14, which is just over the xiphoid process and 7 cun superior to the navel on the midline). Or we could instead strike the lungs, which has a great effect, even when it is a light strike.

Liver 13 and the Gall Bladder

When striking to the point known as Liver 13, we are also likely to strike inward to the actual gall bladder, causing great physical damage that requires hospitalization! And there are so many nerves in this whole area that any strike to the front of the trunk, especially to its sides, is very dangerous. This is why many of the dim-mak "experts" are able to cause certain damage when striking to so-called points. Most of the time they are either striking to nerve points or to physical portions of the body that are highly reactive to being struck.

· · · · ·

All of the above shows that one really must know the difference between dim-mak points, nerve points, and purely physical points on the human body. If, for instance, a teacher says that he strikes nerve points in the neck, ask which ones. Many so-called masters of the martial arts are simply unable to tell us exactly what it is they are hitting. They get a result, of course, but they cannot explain why. This is important, because we as martial arts instructors must tell people about the dangers of showing off, using point strikes to knock people out, and so on.

Fight Like a Wild Animal

After the release of my first book on dim-mak, I received many letters asking for more information on the triune brain and, more specifically, the reptilian part of this brain.

Since my ideas on this were published, others have written to say that they, too, have come across this part of the brain. One person visited a part of Borneo where a native priest was able to place young men into trances that caused them to be like wild boars and allowed them to enter their reptilian brains. This was a rite of manhood, and its purpose was to enable the young men to understand the animal world by becoming animals themselves. While in the reptilian brain, these men were able to do things that humans could not do, like eating a plant commonly eaten by the boar that is so high in arsenic that it would normally kill any human being. Because they were like the wild boar at the time, they were not affected.

We in the martial arts can enter this trancelike state without the help of an external party. The physical manifestation of it is sometimes called qi power. The person who is in this state seems to have some supernatural power, like someone who is mad and requires many men to control him. We learn to use our bodies to cause this reptilian-mind state. When we begin training for this, much emphasis is placed upon what the body is doing physically. But after some time, the physical movements become less important and the mind takes over. We are then able to go into this internal state more easily. All of taiji training is geared toward achieving this state of mind, with the forms themselves beginning quite physically and, after many years, becoming almost nonphysical, with more emphasis on the internal movement of energy.

THE WILD ANIMAL WITHIN

If two people are fighting and both have the ability to go into the reptilian brain, the larger of the two will win. However, if the smaller of the two has been trained in non-human techniques, those that have become subconscious and are very dangerous, then he will win. This is because, although both are able to turn themselves into animals, one's way of fighting is far greater than the other's.

You're pretty strong, and you probably think you are able to handle yourself. Yet you are confronted by a pit bull, and all of your training, all of your energy, falls out of your bum, as you become a quivering wreck, unable to even move, let alone do anything about it. When you think about it, the pit bull is not very big, and really, one good jab on the nose will send him running—or one good kick to the throat will stop him dead. So why do we back off? It's because the animal's oncoming pure aggressive energy is much more than a mere human is able to cope with. Physically, we could beat the animal, but the brain tells us to run.

The pit bull is what we try to become in the internal martial arts. We have the means to become that wild animal mentally and physically, so that when we are attacked we cause the attacker to feel as if he has just opened the door on a raging wild animal. This is not a technique wherein we merely *act* like an animal or imitate its movements, etc. Through certain mental and physical actions, we actually *become* the wild animal. The techniques that we have learned over the years and practiced until they have become subconscious are now used by the brain and body in a "subconscious terrorizing" of our opponent. In order to understand exactly how this works, we must know about the triune brain.

The Triune Brain

Science now tells us that we do not have only one brain inside our heads. We actually have three. As each evolutionary or "creative-evolutionary phase" (depending upon what you believe) took place, a new brain was juxtaposed to the old one. And so, by the time our human brain was in place, the Creator, or evolution, had gone through two other brains. These were not as advanced as the modern human brain, of course, but they still play an important part in our lives.

The *reptilian brain* is the oldest of the three brains, and it is this one that we are concerned with in the internal arts. This is the brain that all reptiles have today, and it is the "survival brain" where humans are concerned. Look at the crocodile; he does not plan his self-defense. He does not think, "I'll just wait until this person comes within range and then pounce." He just does it through sheer instinct. He has no expression, no fear, just survival mechanisms millions of years old. He just does what he has to in order to survive.

The reptile does not see too well, either. It just sees shapes of color. This provides us with some insight into the reptilian brain. We humans tend to use our full-focus vision. So when someone attacks us, we "look" at him; we try to focus upon the attacker's fist as it comes for us. The reptile, on the other hand, does not even see the attacker's peripheral; he just bites at anything that he sees. We, too, have a brain that works in this way; we just have to know how to get into it, as it has probably been sitting dormant since we were about 5 years old.

The *mammalian brain* is the middle brain and is the one used by mammals other than humans. Those animals also have the reptilian brain, but they are able to go into it subconsciously when they need to survive.

The *human brain* is the highest, "logical thinking" brain. Survival methods do not need to be "logical." If we use logical human methods against some raving lunatic, we lose.

So in our heads we actually still have the reptilian brain, and it is there for our survival. Fact is, though, that we have become so human and reliant upon the skills needed for modern twentieth-century living that we have forgotten how to make use of this brain.

In the martial arts, we have certain postures whereby we can bring the reptilian brain into action. Look at the old silver-back gorilla's back. He does not have an "S"-shaped back like ours, but rather a "C"-shaped back. Look at a cat or dog. When it becomes necessary for survival, the back will curve into a "C" shape. This position is the key to the survival brain, or reptilian brain, and its use.

The classics are an integral part of understanding the reptilian brain and the "C" back. Trouble is, many people read them from a book and, with the book in one hand, try to emulate what the author was trying to say some hundreds

Figure 130

Figure 131

Figure 132

of years back. They end up with something like what is shown in Figure 130: "Okay, quick, attack me now!" The classics say that the back must be vertical (plumb) and erect, the shoulders must be loose and hanging, and the chest must be concave with the buttocks tucked under. We are told that this was merely to give us some physical advantage in our stance. But this was actually part of the Chinese way of keeping the secrets from us. Look at the "C"` back in Figure 131. Isn't this what the classics were talking about when they referred to the qi "lifting the back?" Assuming this posture causes the qi to "rise up the back," it will give us the "C" back and, in turn, the reptilian brain. Now, if we also make use of p'eng/ hinge, the posture is complete, and we are able to make use of the full reptilian brain. (*P'eng* and *hinge* are Chinese words that indicate the position of the arms. One arm is held in a p'eng, or ward-off position, while the other is held like a hinge, as in Figure 132.) This is the physical part of the "survival way," or the way in which we train the mind and the body to survive street attacks.

In this posture everything is covered; all we have to do is to move in at the precise

Figure 133

time of attack (fig. 133). And we will do this because we *have* to, as this is what the reptilian brain tells us. You never see an animal backing off when attacked. It will move in to reattack in order to survive.

Using the reptilian brain, we actually become like the animal; the qi is up and we are subconsciously defending ourselves. We want to fight. (In fact, when I hold classes for my senior students, it is quite a difficult job to stop them from doing damage to each other when they use this reptilian brain method.) When the crocodile is just lying there minding his own business and something moves in the bushes, it's like a needle in his side bothering him. As this object, this blur that he cannot focus on, moves toward him, he becomes agitated. When it is within his field of defense, he attacks, because the movement has become too bothersome.

When you can make use of the triune brain by going into this posture of the "C" back and using "eagle vision" (covered in detail in my first book on dim-mak), every movement people make bothers you. It really agitates you, and you want to attack. Even the slightest movement is registered as a large movement. Because you are using what is known as "small peripheral vision" or eagle vision, your visual field is far greater than focus vision. The person using this vision is able to see behind him and greatly to the sides.

There is not much difference between normal standing and the "C" back reptilian brain position. The major difference is in the eyes, which are the mirrors to the inner self. The eyes, in most cases, are enough to stop any potential attacker. You know simply by looking into the eyes of a dog whether or not it is going to eat you! It is the same with us. When we use the third brain, the eyes are generally enough to stop the attack before it has occurred.

PEOPLE CAN'T FIGHT, ANIMALS SURVIVE

There are those who have plodded along with their martial art, really trying to find out what it is all about, with the basic idea that it should be for defense and not for seeing who is the better tournament fighter. It's about "a way of living," of learning about ourselves and learning to help one another, not becoming world champ or satisfying our egos. We should be distinguishing between those who wish to do "boxing in the ring" and those who do the martial arts. (Perhaps those sports people need their own magazine, so that the real martial artists are not mistaken for them.)

Street survival does not happen the way it happens in the ring in a so-called full-contact match. I say "so-called" because there *are no* full-contact matches, at least not legal ones. We have to look at the reason people fight—mostly because of ego or wanting to win money or a trophy, or because it's part of their grading. *This is not survival.* We have to look at why animals fight and how they fight if we are to survive in the street.

Animals are not in control; they react to what is happening to them. An animal does not use techniques; its whole body is involved in the survival effort. Every muscle and ligament is being used, not just a paw or set of teeth. The whole body and an energy that seems to come from nowhere give that animal an aggression that scares even the largest human being.

This is how we are taught to fight to survive in the internal martial arts. We learn certain classic sayings that, when implemented, turn us into raving animals.

Bagwa Palm

What we are told to do in bagwazhang, for instance, is to spread the fingers tightly with a concave palm. The purpose of holding the palm in this position is not so that it can be used more effectively as a weapon, but rather to enable us to summon this animal aggression, or raise the qi up the back. This physical positioning of the palm seems to turn a normally placid human being into a raving lunatic! So when we are attacked, we use the palms in this way not to fight with (although we do use this configuration), but rather to gain the extreme yang energy needed to reattack. (Yang energy is sometimes likened to aggression without the anger.)

"C" Back

In taiji, we have a somewhat more complicated method of gaining this extreme yang energy, and that is the "C" back. It is the same back that *all* animals have when they are in a survival mode. Look at a cat, a dog, even a chicken. When attacked, they all do things with their backbones to gain this survival energy. Even sharks arch their backs when threatened or are about to attack. Gorillas naturally have this "C"-shaped back all the time, but humans have to gain it, as we have "S"-shaped backs.

Fa-Jing

The literal translation of fa-jing is "explosive energy."

The closest that I can get to an analogy is a sneeze or an orgasm—either male or female (not that I would know about the latter, but I guess they feel pretty much the same). The whole body shakes, thrusting out the fist or other attacking weapon. The centrifugal force generated by the body is so great that all one has to do is to place the arm into the right position and let the body do the rest. We learn to "connect" the arms to the torso so that when the waist moves with great power and speed, the arm follows suit.

Of course, the arms are connected to the torso, but normally we use adverse muscles and tension to prevent the peripherals from "going with" the body. We *try* to punch, rather than allowing the fist to be thrust outward by the violent turning action of the waist. If the arms are relaxed, on the other hand, then they will be thrown out automatically. It's like throwing something into a revolving fan: the throw need not be that powerful; however, when the thing hits the fan, it is thrown out with great power. This is fa-jing. Only we do it with the body.

Figure 134

STREET SURVIVAL METHODS

When someone attacks you or strikes out with something toward your face, you automatically cover up, as in Figure 134. In the internal arts, rather than simply using an automatic reaction of covering up, we learn to make this our survival position by training to change it to an attack mode. Instead of going backward in a yin mode, we use certain body positioning to bring out that yang attack energy so that we not only put up our hands but also attack with those same hands into only three targets.

The Three Targets

The three targets we attack to are as follows:

1) the eyes
2) the neck (comprising the Stomach 9 points on the sides of the neck and Conceptor Vessel 22 in the pit of the neck)
3) under the nose to Governor Vessel 26, which is a dim-mak death point

The Three Weapons

We use the following three weapons to attack the above targets:

1) the tips of the fingers (fig. 135)
2) the "knife edge" of the palm (fig. 136)
3) the "heel of the palm" (fig. 137)

In Figure 135, I have used my fingers to attack to the eyes, as the opponent has attacked with both hands toward my face. My forearms have opened up his arms, blocking them outward, thus leaving

Figure 135

Figure 136

Figure 137

his eyes open to the attack. With a little more training, we can go beyond just poking our fingers into his eyes and use simple, natural movements that give us the best possible chance in a street survival situation. These techniques all come from the natural human reaction of covering up (i.e., being yin) upon being startled.

For instance, rather than bringing your palms forward into his eyes with extreme yang energy, you might turn slightly and strike into the carotid artery area of St 9, as in Figure 136. This will cause instant KO (as well as death if done with enough power). Here I have used the second weapon, the knife edge. The initial move of "opening him up" with my forearms is the same as that used when the eyes were the target.

You could use basically that same movement to attack the Gv 26 point, as depicted in Figure 137. Here, I have used the heel of the palm to strike upward into Gv 26. Again, the initial block is exactly the same as for the previous two targets. Or, again using the fingers, you could attack to Cv 22, as in Figure 138.

Figure 138

We use the same basic movement for all three targets and weapons; it is just a matter of using the target and weapon most suitable for the moment. Again, you do not have to put in years of training for basic self-defense using dim-mak; just these three methods will enable you to defend yourself by attacking to the most deadly areas of your attacker's body.

HOW IT WORKS INTERNALLY

These natural techniques give us the best possible chance in the street without our having to learn a whole martial art for 20 years. And this is what martial arts should be about.

When a human is startled, just as when an animal is startled, the kidneys release extreme energy into the body. The kidneys store this yang energy, or qi, for when it is needed, and it works upon the adrenal gland. For a short time after it is released, we seem to have more power than normal. The animals have never lost their way of subconsciously converting this energy into attack energy. By contrast, when we are startled, because of our soft Western life-styles, we become yin and tend to cower to avoid being hit. We become afraid. The internal arts teach us to reverse the yin energy to yang attack energy, so that when we are attacked, the attacker is confronted not by a docile human but a raving lunatic. We take the human phenomenon that occurs when we are startled and combine it with the body posturing of the internal arts, such as the "C" back and the "bagwa palm," and this enables us to be like the animals when attacked.

We learn forms, katas, two-person exercises, and so on, to give us the balance and timing necessary for street survival, then we combine them with natural body positioning to defend ourselves using the animal inside—and we all have one somewhere.

Triggers

Our brain works on triggers. We have internal triggers, which we are born with, and external triggers, which we must learn. Animals have mainly internal triggers and are able to survive by themselves not too long after birth. Humans have mainly "learned" triggers and are not able to survive until long after birth. For instance, waking up usually triggers the desire to clean our teeth or go to the bathroom, etc. These are learned triggers. Martial artists and those who wish to learn about self-defense at a survival level must learn certain triggers. Set patterns of natural movements—those which flow with life in general, such as in arts like taiji and bagwa—are easier to learn as external triggers than those that are rigid and not naturally flowing, such as sometimes occur in the "hard"-style martial arts.

After many years of training, every move, every posture becomes a trigger that causes something internal to happen; it is a small switch that turns something on. To use an analogy, in the internal arts it is also essential that we learn about health and nutrition. So when people come to me for advice and I tell them this, they look at me with astonishment and say something like, "Surely there's more to it than that!" or "Surely, one little cream cake won't hurt—I haven't had one for days." I tell them that the body is like a battery. It is the "body electric" with many different currents flowing around it all the time, otherwise known as qi. When we wish to turn on a light, we do not fiddle with the light itself, but rather we turn on a tiny switch that causes something miraculous to happen—let there be light! It's the same with the human body. It's not the cream cake itself, but rather the switch that the cream cake turns on that does the damage! Even a minute fragment of that cake turns on the same switch as would 10 cream cakes.

So when people say to me, "Wow, it doesn't look like one could get much from those few slow movements," I answer the same: *It's not the movement or the posture that does the work, but the switch that particular posture or movement turns on internally that matters.* Thus, the most minute movement could be doing huge things to our minds internally, and our bodies externally. By contrast, someone who works out at the gym sees some great physical changes over a relatively short period of time, but almost nothing internally—no switches. This is the difference between the internal and the external martial arts.

If we learn a martial art that forces unnatural movement upon us, no matter how long we work at it, that movement will never become a trigger or be a natural reflex action. When we need it most, then, it will be lost in the heat of the moment because it has not become subconscious. If, however, we learn movements that are natural, each movement will become a trigger with practice. Then, when we are confronted by some raving lunatic who wishes to do us damage, we will react with the correct trigger to turn us into a wild animal. We will be able to defend ourselves, not because we practiced a technique for many years but because we trained to learn triggers and our movement will become subconscious. We now have the mind of an animal when needed.

All of internal arts training is geared toward learning triggers; even training methods that seemingly have nothing to do with the martial arts are there for a reason.

Everything that animals or humans do is related to these triggers. Something sets us off. It could be a smell or subconscious eye contact, but all of our emotions are set off by such triggers. These triggers usually come from outside, but sometimes we are able to control the triggers from within to cause our brains to do something. In the case of self-defense, we can cause our brains to go into reptilian mode by using simple body language. In this way, even the smallest of humans is able to become like the wild animal and defend himself. Of course, he must first of all be trained in some form of fighting. This is where the martial arts have it all over other forms of self-defense. It's all there for us to make use of. The katas, the forms, the two-person training methods—all lead us to the no-mind or reptilian brain state. And the more training we have done, then the more able we are to make use of the reptilian brain for survival.

There are a couple of old Chinese martial arts sayings that are important for the martial artist who wishes to use his or her art for self-defense:

> • *If you use a technique, you will lose.* This has been proven over and over again. We see the trained black belt who, when he is finally attacked in the street by a good streetfighter, is defeated in the first few seconds. The black belt has learned *techniques* but has not taken his art to the internal level where his techniques become nontechniques. His mind must react without thinking, and his body must be able to react to what the mind is telling him instantly and subconsciously. This black belt is defeated because he has none of the above. However, the person who has been able to turn his mar-

tial art into a survival art will survive because he is no longer relying upon physical, human technique. Animals do not use techniques! A dog does not think, as he is being rushed at by that bloody great German shepherd, "Now, I'll just wait until he is a bit closer, and then I will do a leg sweep and put a paw lock onto his rear left paw, thus causing Heart 5 to drain all of his energy, so that I can then bite him on the neck." No, the dog simply relies upon his internal switches to cause him to react to what the other dog is doing to him. He has already done the training when he was young, play-fighting with his mother and brothers and sisters. He no longer relies upon technique, but only internal mind. He attacks as the other dog attacks and reacts to what is being done to him. (Then afterward, after one dog is beaten up or dead, our little doggy becomes little Benjie again and we pat him. When just a few seconds before, he was a lunatic!) This is the same with all animals—they just react internally.

• *Do what he does not want you to do.* When someone is attacking us, he expects certain things to happen. He also has certain triggers built in because of his many fights in the street, etc. He wants and expects us to do certain things. He wants us to stand there and take his punch and then reattack with another punch or kick. This is what he is used to. The attacker does not want us to do something that he is not used to, like moving forward and not backward as he attacks.

Some people are naturally gifted in being raving lunatics. Others of us have to learn to be so. From the internal arts, we have some training methods that lend themselves to fighting like the wild animal.

**Internal Training Method No. 1
(To Do What He Does Not Want Us To Do):
"V"-Stepping**

If someone attacks us with a punch, he expects us to be there when the punch arrives. He would not have thrown the punch if he thought we would not be there! So our first training is to learn to move in and not back (a little to the

Figure 139

side, of course). This is called "V"-stepping, and it is what animals do. They will wait until the very last split second and then move to the side to move in. In my first book on dim-mak, I included methods to gain entry, and this is part of the "not doing what he wants us to do." Here I will give you a "V"-stepping exercise that will help you learn to move in and to the side as you defend/attack.

Your partner stands in front of you. You are using eagle vision. The very instant your partner moves in to kick you with a straight kick to your midsection, you step with either foot to either side in a "V," as in Figure 139. Your back leg must be against a wall and must not come off the wall, so that when you recover your front foot, it too will go against the wall, ready to step again or for the other foot to step again in a "V" to the other side.

Internal Training Method No. 2: Double-Attacking

Just to get the idea of not doing what the attacker wants us to do, here is another training method. This one people really do not like when it happens, as they just do not want it to happen this way. You throw a right hook at your partner, who will perhaps block it using a strong p'eng block, as in Figure 140. Now, he has successfully blocked your punch, and he *knows* that you will now reattack with the left fist or kick him, etc. He does not want or expect you to attack again with the same hand, so you do! Immediately after he has blocked your fist, he will subconsciously slack off the power, as this is what his internal switches have taught him.

Figure 140

Now, in order to do this correctly, you must have fa-jing. This is because we need to be able to reattack with the same fist from a very short distance without drawing it back, and still have great power. So now the whole body reacts internally and externally, as when sneezing, and the right fist is again thrust into his

Figure 141

Figure 142

Figure 143

now weakened defense, as in Figure 141. (Sneezing, literally, is the same body explosion as fa-jing. You cannot just sneeze using your nose! Your whole body reacts uncontrollably.)

Internal Training Method No. 3: Nun Offers Food

Another excellent internal technique from bagwa that has this "not doing what he wants" attitude is called "nun offers food." The posture is shown in Figure 142. This requires some movement from the center, from whence, as any internal person knows, all movement must come. Again, you throw a hook punch with your right hand, and he blocks using the p'eng block, as in Figure 143. However, just before—and I mean a thousandth of a second before—your hand touches his, you duck your right shoulder under his hand, as in Figure 144. The position of your body (coiled) gives you the power to bring that right palm right up under his defense to attack his neck. The left hand is there as a back-up, as in Figure 145. This he did not want you to do. He knew that he would block your attack, but it is not there to be blocked, and before he realizes it, you have your palm in his neck.

A good martial artist is not always a good fighter. Some of the best fighters have never seen the inside of a dojo. No matter how many techniques you know, how good you are at kata or form, you are not necessarily able to defend yourself. You still have to learn to fight. My friend Graham Noble from England, a martial artist and journalist, has always said that it does not matter how many points you know or where and when you strike

Figure 144

Figure 145

them—you still have to know how to smash his face in or take out his leg! And when you know how to do this, you don't need points any more.

PUSH HANDS:
A TRIUNE-BRAIN TRAINING EXERCISE

This is the best exercise for learning about the triune brain. But I am not talking about the normal type of push hands that just about everyone and his dog is doing, the "p'eng, lu jai and arn" routine. (This type of push hands is that which most people consider to be normal in taiji.) I am talking about a more sophisticated set of two-person movements that is sometimes called joining arms.

Actually, there are no pushes in taiji or any of the internal arts. Why push? He only comes back and beats the hell out of you. Why pull? There are also no pulls in taiji. The correct words here are "strikes and negative strikes." This is where we are taught not to pull or lock an arm, but rather to violently jerk the wrist, thus activating the heart and lung points on the wrist, which makes the body weaker and more vulnerable to a more devastating attack. Pull someone as hard as you like. What does this do? He is now behind you to attack from behind! So someone attacks you and you push with your most powerful push, and he goes over several tables and lands on the floor, only to get back up and attack again.

The garden variety of taiji practitioner says, "But now he knows that I mean business!" Bullshit, mate! He just gets angry and floors you.

We are able to use advanced p'eng/hinge push hands in everything we learn in the internal arts. This type of push hands teaches us how to fight, and not how to push and pull. It shows you the dim-mak points to strike and drills you so that it all becomes subconscious and you do not have to think about it. You don't think, "Oh, here comes a straight right, so I'll use this set-up point and this major strike." The body and mind react to the attack and act accordingly without your ever having to think about it. The dim-mak point that you strike to depends upon the shape of your body at the time of attack.

This type of push hands also teaches us about never striking two or more points at the same time. Every point strike and its indications are medically proven. We know that in order to affect the heart, then we must strike the points, or the heart itself, on what is known as the "positive stroke." This is when the ventricles (the left in particular is operational) are contracting and the heart is at its most vulnerable. Most dim-mak strikes affect the heart in some way to weaken the body. This is why we always strike with two or more

Figure 146

Figure 147

point strikes, so that we are certain to get the heartbeat somewhere on its most important stroke. The internal arts have a lot more to offer than a bit of relaxation and stretching. There's a whole world of science out there in the martial arts, and we can make use of this information to turn our martial art, no matter what style, into a devastating fighting art or self-defense method.

Of course if you do not wish to go through all that training, you could just ask a friend of mind who's "in the know," shown in Figures 146 and 147. (And, yes, it's real.)

The Dim-Mak Claw

5

What has happened to taiji over the years is not exceptional or unusual; the martial arts in general have experienced a similar erosion. As the various systems moved further and further away from their founders, separated by time, many of the hidden movements became vague or were lost. Many reasons have been attributed to this, one of which is that students left their instructors and opened their own schools, thinking that they knew the whole system, when they really only knew a portion of it. As time moved on, the original founders took fewer and fewer students and, because of a general lack of dedication, fewer students were receiving the whole system. The various martial arts became increasingly vague, with so many claiming to be the main students of the many founders of the different systems after those founders had died.

Nowadays, we have many different kung-fu systems, but only a handful of them are the original systems, and even fewer people have actually received the whole training of those systems that are still intact.

With dim-mak (taijiquan/t'ai chi), however, this degradation has been even more profound, with so many instructors only ever learning the initial slow kata or form and then claiming mastery and opening schools. They, in turn, teach what little they know to others, who go out and teach the even smaller amount that they know, and so it goes. It has come to the point where instructors of taiji are only teaching it as a form of relaxation, like yoga. But unlike yoga, taiji provides no benefits if one does not learn it as it was originally intended and, more importantly, *how it was originally taught*. Today, the dim-mak in taiji is not even recognized, even by the so-called most senior of the world's masters. About all they get to in the self-defense area is the use of each posture as a self-defense movement. It's like just sitting in a Porsche without actually turning the ignition key!

The "dim-mak claw" is something that has traveled the long road and has been changed and renamed until it is no longer recognizable in taiji. It is something that we do in the taiji form all the time, but which others know nothing about. We are told by most instructors, to "hold the beautiful hand" or by some to "hold the tile palm hand" (fig. 148). Many have said it has something to do with the flow of qi (whenever an instructor is in doubt about a question from a student at a seminar, the stock answer is that it has something to do with "the flow"!) or that it helps us to relax. Actually, the "tile palm

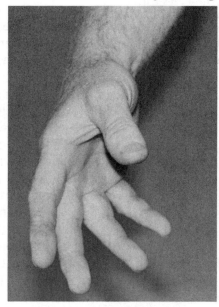

Figure 148

hand" or "beautiful hand" has a much more sinister reason for being. Each finger of the tile palm hand is used to strike to certain dim-mak points, mainly on the face, but it is also applied to other parts of the body, as in clawing or grabbing, in order to attack points. The fingers are held in this way so that we do not have to think about striking to specific points. Instead, we just strike and the fingers are in the correct position for striking to at least four or five important points.

The whole hand is held in such a way that, as we strike, the fingers will be relaxed enough to spring into the points and will not have to be thrust into them. Thrusting with a tense hand blocks the flow of adverse qi from going into the points. (I'm talking advanced dim-mak striking here, not just the striking of the points that will always work, regardless of how advanced one is in the internal arts.) Sometimes, in order to damage the points, we need to put in adverse energy. In doing this, we are able to upset or slow down the flow of energy within the attacker's body, rather than just causing a knockout or making him fall down.

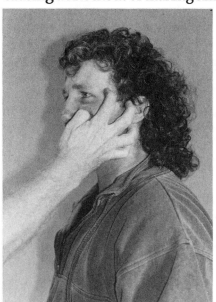

In taiji, the palms are always held in this way. When we are attacked, it becomes a subconscious reaction to use the fingers in this way. It is quicker than using specific techniques and also does more damage.

THE POINTS

Each finger of the dim-mak claw attacks a specific point on the face. Figures 149 and 150 show the positioning of each finger on the face.

Figure 149

Dim-Mak Claw Point No. 1

The thumb attacks to Stomach 3 (St 3), situated just under the cheekbone in line with the pupil. A strike to St 3 has the effect of draining qi from the lower abdomen. This will cause one to feel quite nauseated. The heavier the strike, the greater the sickly feeling, to the point of forcing the recipient to sit down. One is able to strike this point all by itself by

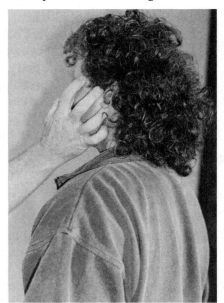

Figure 150

poking the index and second fingers upward into the cheekbone. It is used in this way when one is only trying to *control* an attacker and the situation is not too serious (fig. 151).

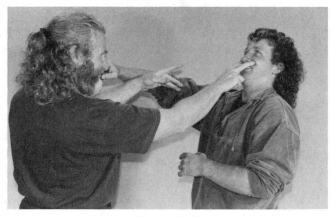

Figure 151

Dim-Mak Claw Point No. 2

The index finger attacks Gall Bladder 1. This point, in the outside corner of each eye and just over the eye socket bone, will cause a knockout, as will any gall-bladder point. The direction for this strike is straight in.

Dim-Mak Claw Point No. 3

The second finger attacks Gall Bladder 2 (Gb 2). Just forward of the ear notch, there is a hollow that's created when the mouth is opened. This is the location of Gb 2, which is another knockout point because of its action on the carotid sinus.

Dim-Mak Claw Point No. 4

The fourth finger attacks Triple Warmer 17. Tw 17 is normally a death point and *can* be so when using the dim-mak claw. However, when used in conjunction with the other points attacked by the claw, it generally becomes a controlling point and a set-up point. It drains energy from the "seat of power," or the lungs, when struck straight in, so the attacker no longer has any energy with which to fight. This point is located directly behind the ear lobe, a little below the hollow, but not below the lowest edge of the ear lobe.

Dim-Mak Claw Point No. 5

The small finger attacks Small Intestine 17 (Si 17), located just under the jaw bone at its furthest edge (away from the attacker). Also an energy drainage point for the lungs, Si 17 causes the person to lose his desire to carry on with the fight.

The dim-mak claw can be used in many other ways. It does not always have to be held exactly as in Figure 149. The palm can be used with the small finger upward. If someone attacks with a straight right, for instance, you might slam the Neigwan point on the inside of his right forearm with your right palm, as in Figure 152. Then that same hand rebounds off and into the side of his face (fig.

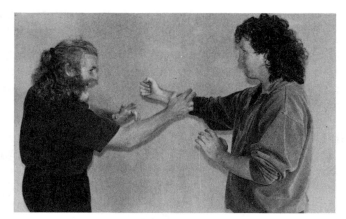

Figure 152

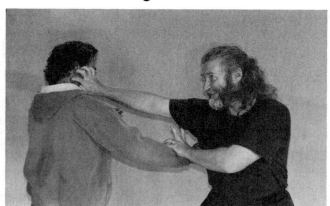

Figure 153

Figure 154

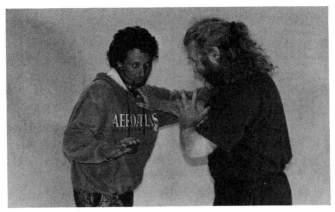

Figure 155

153). Each finger has again struck one of the five points mentioned above, so the effect is the same.

The claw does not have to be used only against the face points, either. It might be used to block a left hook (fig. 154) and then slam downward with a grabbing/pulling motion into the Stomach 11 and 12 points on top of the clavicle. Striking St 12 has the effect of taking the opponent's will to fight away (draining his seat of power), and striking to the vagus nerve at St 11 affects his heart rate (fig. 155).

Tearing, grabbing, and squeezing are all part of the claw's action. You might again block a left hook punch, as in Figure 154, which leaves the claw free to strike and

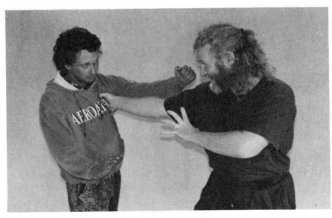

Figure 156

squeeze to Stomach 15, on the pectoral, and Gall Bladder 22 (Gb 22), under the arm, as in Figure 156. St 15, when attacked in this way, causes the person to lose his fighting energy, while Gb 22 is a knockout point. You must turn your body away from your attacker (i.e., your torso must turn to your left, as in the photo) to gain the necessary thrust for this strike.

The dim-mak claw is constantly "at the ready." We use it when we are performing the solo forms. We use it when we are practicing the pushing hands exercises from taiji.

Figure 157

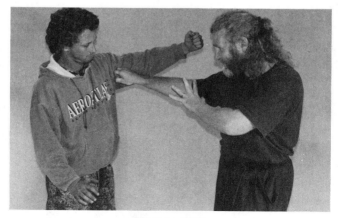

Figure 158

We use it to grab the wrists of an attacker after the initial attack in order to control him.

The dim-mak claw works with the "tiger paw fist. " If we throw a punch after the palm has been held in the dim-mak claw, the fingers will close so that we now have the tiger paw fist. So it is an easy thing to change from claw to fist. For instance, if someone attacks with a left hook, you might attack the inside of his arm at the elbow crease with the dim-mak claw (fig. 157). Then, as your body swivels to your left, your palm turns into a tiger paw to attack to

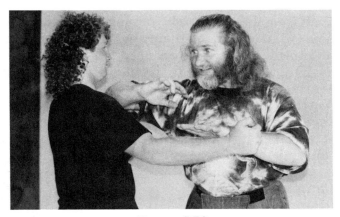

Figure 159

Figure 160

nerve points where the biceps meets with the triceps on the inside of the upper arm (fig. 158).

The claw can also be used with other techniques. For example, the attacker might attack with a right hook. You would block his attack with your left palm as your right elbow attacked to his neck (fig. 159). Now your right claw is free to come back to attack to vital points in his neck (fig. 160).

WAYS TO TRAIN THE DIM-MAK CLAW

Apart from the normal taiji training of push hands and *chee-sau* (sticking hands), there are a number of ways to train the claw. This training is used not only to develop strong hands, but mainly to develop speed and timing while using the claw.

We strike to the hard mitt with the tips of the fingers, making a cracking sound. The person holding the mitt must feel an energy going into it, but the mitt must not be moved too far away, as this is a push. You must hold your hand only inches away from the mitt to begin with, and then attack so that the whole wrist whips into it and then away with the rebound.

Use a piece of cylindrical wood or a similar object, about 2.5 inches in diameter. A wooden dummy (a la wing chun) is ideal for this, only the arm must be a little larger in diameter. First slam

Figure 161

Figure 162

the object upward, as in Figure 161. Then, without stopping and without losing the speed gained from this attack, your palm does a circle to get around on top of the cylinder, then grabs with a pulling motion toward you (fig. 162).

Have someone throw different types of attacks at you. You should be able to follow up every block with the claw. For instance, you might block his left jab with your forearm, as in Figure 163, and then, in an instant, bring your right claw underneath to attack to his lower body (fig. 164). Any type of attack can be blocked and countered in this way using the claw.

Figure 163

Figure 164

Try going from claw to tiger paw fist in response to your partner's different attacks. Keep it nice and easy at first, but as you become more competent and the movement becomes more natural, speed up the action.

Knockout and Controlling Points for Law Enforcement

A s a law enforcement officer for the past 10 years, I have looked for an effective martial art that would assist me in my job with minimum risk of injury to myself and the people I deal with. This, as you know, is not an easy endeavor.

So when I met Erle Montaigue about 4 years ago, I was pleasantly surprised to find someone who could practice what the classics in taiji discussed. He has a true knowledge of the fighting aspects and the ability to explain them.

It has been both an honor and a pleasure to call him a friend and teacher over the past several years. He has enriched and expanded my knowledge of taiji, and has shown me that it is one of the greatest martial arts ever invented. In this chapter, Master Montaigue takes the mystery out of the art and teaches law enforcement officers realistic methods of surviving street attacks. His approach is not to teach techniques, but to show the natural way of fighting, using the whole body to defend yourself.

I hope Erle's teaching will help you as much as it has me.

—Al Krych

NOTE: As with any of the information in my books on dim-mak, I stress that it is *extremely dangerous* to experiment with the following points. While anyone can cause an instant knockout by simply pushing backward on the vagus nerve area, please do not do this just to impress your friends, as you could end up in *gaol* (jail) for manslaughter!

I have a number of law enforcement people come to my workshops and order the videos. These people are especially interested in the points that control the body, and this includes the knockout points. Because they are working with danger every day and need to be able to control those who would cause harm to either themselves or others, they need to know which points work the best in these situations.

The choice of points to use depends upon what kind of attack is being used. So if, for instance, your hand were around the back of the attacker's neck because he rushed at you to try to grapple, you would not try to knock him out using St 9 on the front of the neck. Instead, you would use a light tap to a neurological shutdown point at the back of the neck to put your attacker down. Your hand is already there. He does not see it coming and does not even know that he has been struck until he wakes up on the ground or in your arms.

KNOCKOUT POINTS

There are several ways to knock someone out. Neurological shutdown and dim-mak point striking are two.

When we strike to neurological shutdown (NS) points, we are affecting first the brain's perception of what is happening to the body and, consequently, the whole nervous system. The brain either thinks that something really dire has happened, or it does not know quite what has happened, so it shuts the whole nervous system down.

The receiver's recovery will depend upon whether we have struck with great force or light force, but his brain will shut the system down regardless. The NS strikes cause this phenomenon to happen only in human beings, not in animals, and there are only four NS points on the human body.

A good grappler has no chance against someone who knows about neurological shutdown. Now, normally, I would not even allow a grappler to get close enough that he could get his hands on me, but at my workshops, I allow someone who is good at grappling (or wrestling, judo, etc.) to come in close and actually try to throw me, or do whatever he wishes. Rather than try to grapple with him, I allow him to come really close and then tap him on the back of the neck on the rear NS point, and he doesn't even know he has been struck until he is looking up from the floor. Now, I only ever have to do this once. I don't have to repeat this at my workshops, as everyone there has seen how effective it is. And unlike others who do similar techniques, I explain exactly how it is done and that anyone can do it.

But don't do it! It takes many years of practice before one can do it without causing irreparable damage to the nervous system. (This point is discussed further in the main section on NS later on in this chapter.) Your hand is around the back, so he doesn't even see it coming, making this a great technique for defending against grapplers.

I am often asked if there are any sure, safe ways to put someone down. No. All strikes that attack either the nervous system or the circulatory system or the dim-mak system (acupuncture points) are dangerous. However, if there is a relatively safe way, compared to the others, then it would have to be the "neuroshutdown." What does this do? There are certain points on the human body that react in a certain way when struck. I don't know why we have these points; they are just there. Attacks to these points are not nerve strikes per se, but they do affect the nervous system and, depending upon the amount of force used, cause the body to fall down for a couple of seconds or more.

I must stress here, though, that you have to be able to use these points in a realistic situation—not just strike someone standing in front of you. In workshops I have people attack me and then show them. The points work even better this way, as the person's energy is up. All that is required is a light tap. If I were to do it without his attacking, it would require more power on my part. (I don't do that, as it obviously becomes more dangerous as the power increases.)

I had two police officers attend one of my workshops in London, and they came to me with a problem. They said that they deal with drunks and drug-crazed idiots all the time and that sometimes these people don't feel pain—a good whack on the nose that causes profuse bleeding, and they don't even feel it! I explained that what we're dealing with here is not actually pain, and that anyone who states, "I give them some pain" does not know real dim-mak. When we use dim-mak we don't give people pain; we strike points that cause human phenomena to occur. (I say "human" because, again, this does not happen in animals.)

When someone is struck at one of these NS points, they wake up on the ground or in my arms and wonder why they are there. They didn't feel the initial strike, nor did they feel any pain. They just dropped, their eyes rolled back, and they were out. Often they accuse someone behind them of hitting them! Often they will not even realize that they have been out, and only when everyone watching tells them what has happened do they believe.

So this was a case where I had to demonstrate on the officers. Obviously, police officers are facing danger constantly, and so they have to know that the points are going to work. If they respond to a call and have to use a point to control the situation and it doesn't work, then they are in trouble.

Because the police officer's attack was straight in with both hands, I used a different NS point. *You have to use the points that are relevant to the attack being thrust upon you.* This time, I simply slapped him on the side of the jaw. (This point is discussed in detail in the main section on NS points further along in this chapter.) For this strike, the long finger is placed just under the side of the jaw where the angle of the jaw is, but it is all five fingers that actually do the damage. In this case, he came in like a ton of bricks with both arms, and I actually turned his power back on him, following up with an attack to a dim-mak point to control his body.

The great thing about most of the NS knockouts is that there's no mumbo jumbo involved, such as having to first know the set-up points, or how to cross this fire point with this wood point, or how the water point works against the metal point, etc. People who talk about this kind of thing when using these techniques are only doing so because they want us to believe that only they have this knowledge, and they are trying to make it inaccessible to normal people. Really, it's a simple matter of just hitting the points; they work, regardless of the five-element theory and so on. (The-five element theory comes from acupuncture and, in a nutshell, says that in Chinese medicine the five main elements have a destructive cycle; for instance, metal [an element] destroys wood. This, in turn, can be used in treating the internal organs that have the same characteristics as the five elements.)

There are, however, points that are made more effective by striking certain set-up points first, and that's a different story. While the NS points work regardless of set-up points being used, certain dim-mak points are more effective when the set-up points are used.

Knockouts resulting from strikes to dim-mak points are caused mainly by the strike's effect on the carotid sinus. They can also be caused by severe energy drainage from the body. So here, we are not looking at a nervous reaction, but rather a physiological reaction caused either by the slowing or stopping of the heart or by energy drainage.

As mentioned in Chapter 3, quite often when striking these knockout points, we access the nerve points with the same strike. So we get a double reaction.

CONTROLLING POINTS

The controlling points are still dim-mak points, and, as such, will cause death if struck with too much power. However, with less power these points can be used to control a person's body. These points bring about certain physiological reactions that cause the person to either fall down or to stop trying to attack you.

"Doormen" or bouncers can use these to control a drunken person so that he is easier to remove from a club or bar. Law enforcement officers often wish to know of a better way to control someone than hitting him over the head with a nightstick. I show them that all you need to do is press one finger into certain points and the body cannot move; you can just take the attacker out.

The particular point I use to demonstrate this, Controlling Point No. 1 (covered later in this chapter), attacks the lungs, which control a person's will to fight. Take that will away, and the person will do what you want him to. This controlling point is Triple Warmer 17, just at the back of the ear. Some knowledge of acupuncture points is required to utilize it properly. This is an extreme death point when struck hard, but in this instance you use only one finger to attack it, with a push inward and back toward you (assuming that you are standing in front of the attacker).

NEUROLOGICAL SHUTDOWN POINTS

All dim-mak points are death points. However, many can be used with different pressures and angles to cause a knockout to occur. While most of the dim-mak points simply cause death and must be struck with relatively hard pressure, here I will discuss those that are neurological shutdown points. These are dim-mak points that attack nerves and not necessarily acupuncture points, and they can be used for definite and relatively easy knockouts.

Many of the following points are already covered in my first book on dim-mak. However, I will include them

Figure 165

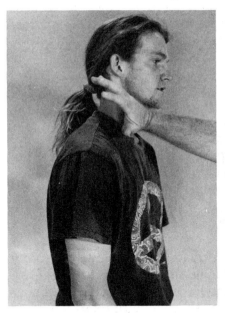

Figure 166

here also and go into them in greater detail.

If I wanted to strike to a *nerve point* in order to damage the arm only, I could strike the ulnaris nerve on the inside of the arm, and the whole arm would become useless. Figure 165 shows the strike and the weapon used.

By contrast, while the *neurological shutdown points* are situated over important nerves, they actually attack the *whole* nervous system and not just the nerve under the strike. The ancient Chinese masters (not necessarily the modern ones) knew about these dim-mak points, calling them "soft points." (They did not have the scientific knowledge that we have today and relied upon experimentation with either each other or with people they did not like to gain this knowledge of the NS points and other dim-mak points.)

For instance, you can strike the front of the neck area and affect a number of different points (both dim-mak and NS). If you hold the palm as in Figure 166 and strike lightly inward against St 9, the person will be knocked out by the action of the carotid sinus. This is a dim-mak point strike. When the blood pressure rises, the pressoreceptors (baroreceptors) inside the carotid sinus act on the cardio-inhibitory center of the brain to send signals via the vagus nerve that cause the heart to slow down or to stop. If the blood pressure is too low, the pressoreceptors simply do not act and so the blood pressure rises again due to reflex acceleration of the heart. This universal relationship between blood pres-

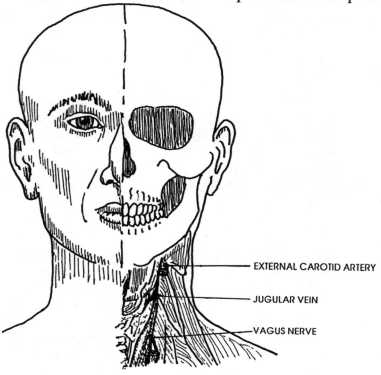

EXTERNAL CAROTID ARTERY

JUGULAR VEIN

VAGUS NERVE

Figure 167

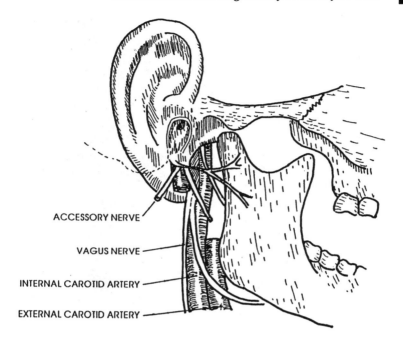

ACCESSORY NERVE

VAGUS NERVE

INTERNAL CAROTID ARTERY

EXTERNAL CAROTID ARTERY

Figure 168

sure and heart rate is called Marey's Law of the Heart. Figure 167 shows the positioning of the vagus nerve, the external carotid artery, and the jugular vein. Figure 168 shows the positioning of the internal carotid artery, the external carotid artery, and the vagus nerve.

NS Point No. 1

Notice that the vagus nerve is situated along the internal carotid artery. But if we place the palm as in Figure 169, with the little finger just forward of the ear lobe, then we will be making a nerve strike to the vagus nerve, provided that the base of the knife edge of the palm is also placed into the notch of the clavicle as shown. This bottom point is Stomach 11 and is the closest to where the vagus nerve comes to the surface. All one has to do to cause the vagus nerve to signal the heart to slow or stop is push inward and bend the vagus nerve, as in Figure 170. The pressure can range from light push to a medium-powered push that forces the person's head backward, depending on the person. In some people, only a rubbing along the vagus nerve is required to cause knockout.

The dangers of striking to the neck are great. In striking to NS

Figure 169

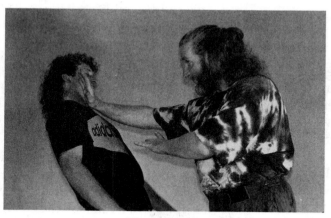

Figure 170

Point No. 1, we can also strike a dim-mak point (St 9) as well as a "blood knockout point." A blood strike is when we simply stop the blood flow to the brain by creasing any of the major arteries and veins that either supply or take blood

Figure 171

Figure 172

away from the brain. If, for instance, we place the palm as in Figure 171, with the whole side of the palm a little further toward the back of the head and the little finger in the hollow below the ear lobe, the result is a blood knockout brought about by the action on the jugular vein. Here is the danger: if we strike NS Point No. 1 with *too much pressure*, because of its vicinity to the vagus nerve, the carotid artery, and the carotid sinus, we will affect all three areas, and *death will be imminent*.

This tells you a little about the relationship between dim-mak point strikes, nerve strikes, and NS strikes.

This strike to NS Point No. 1 can be used before the person has actually grabbed you, which, of course, is the best scenario, as he does not have time even to get a lock on. Figure 172 shows a technique that utilizes this strike. Suppose he

139 ■

just runs at you with both hands. Stretching your fingers to bring up extreme yang qi, you move in and, with the arms slightly curved as shown, strike him in the neck with your right palm as your left palm assists in moving his arms outward. The physics of holding the arms in the curved position provide you with better leverage.

NS Point No. 2

A strike to NS Point No. 2 is very useful, as it can be used against grapplers after they have actually grabbed you. This strike too is over an important nerve, the accessory nerve. This nerve controls, among other things, head and shoulder movement and arises from the first five segments of the spinal cord. Striking the correct part of this nerve will cause a neurological shutdown. The brain does not quite know what has happened and so shuts everything down, just in case!

A word of warning here: If you have not had years of experience in this strike in particular, then DO NOT DO IT! This point is very close to the base of the skull, and in view of the many vital activities controlled by the medulla, a blow to this area is very likely to be fatal. (See Figure 168 for the accessory nerve and Figure 173 for the placement of the palm on the back of the neck.) You can strike this point from a very short distance— sometimes as little as a half an inch—to gain the knockout. Your attacker will not even

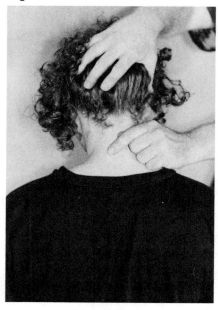

Figure 173

realize your palm is where it is, and by the time he does, it's too late.

It is also interesting that the accessory nerve is connected to the vagus nerve up higher and, in fact, travels for a time in the same sheath. So in striking the accessory, we are also affecting the vagus, thus causing not only neuroshutdown, but heart stoppage as well.

NS Point No. 3

Note the position of the palm in relation to the side of the jaw in Figure 174. The longest finger is just under the jaw, but it is the whole hand that is doing the work. This is the third of the NS points. The direction of the strike must be straight in toward the neck, and we gain our power from what he is doing to us. If it is a heavy strike against us, then our NS strike will be heavy. We use his oncoming power against him.

Take the previous attack, when he came at you with both arms. (This could, of course, be only one arm; the technique is the same.) We literally bounce our right arm off his left forearm, as in Figure 175, and then slam the palm into the side of his jaw (fig. 176). Note that the palm had to be "loaded" to begin with so that we actually struck the inside of his arm at Neigwan, or Pericardium 6 (Pc 6), with a yin-shaped hand, which is full of yang energy. (See fig. 177 for the loading of yin energy and fig. 178 for

Figure 174

Figure 175

Figure 176

Figure 177

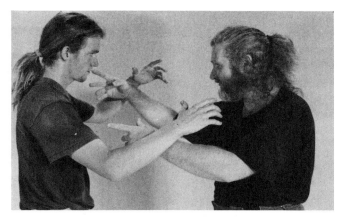

Figure 178

the delivery of it.) When the wrist is flexed, it is said to be full of yin qi. The only work it can do is to explosively flick back the other way and strike with the back of the palm. This is when the yin energy is said to "go into" the point.

Now, the palm is loaded with yang energy, and when it strikes into the jaw, the yang energy is released into the points. So your wrist must flex from bent to limp to flexed as it strikes. This takes a split second. Be sure not to actually block his arm, as you are relying upon the rebound from the strike to his arm for the power for your final strike. You will, of course, block his strike, but you must not be looking to actually block. Rather, you are trying to strike him. This, in turn, turns into a rebound into his face.

The nerve we are dealing with here is the auricularis magnus. This is another strike that will cause the person to go into knockout by its action on the entire nervous system. It must not be a push, however, as when attacking to the vagus nerve. This time it must be a sharp slap.

NS Point No. 4

This area has the eye as its center, the cheekbone as its bottom, and the eyebrow as its top. A slap here causes neurological shutdown in human beings. This is a combination attack to a nerve, a dim-mak point, and receptors

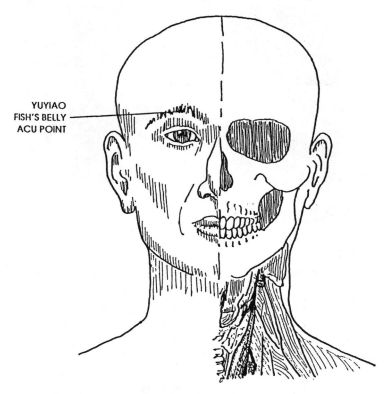

YUYIAO
FISH'S BELLY
ACU POINT

Figure 179

called proprioceptors. The palm knuckles strike to the facial nerve, which runs under the cheekbone, while the finger knuckles strike an extraordinary dim-mak point called Yuyiao, or Fish's Belly, located at the center of the eyebrow (see Fig. 179). The proprioceptors allow us to feel position and movement, control equilibrium, etc. If we place the back of our palm onto the eye area, as shown in Figure 180, we are able to strike to all three areas, causing a neurological shutdown.

A technique that utilizes this particular area would be to slap his arm on the outside, toward us, when he attacks with a straight left, for instance. This is a set-up point for the Yuyiao point. Then, as the wrist is loaded,

Figure 180

i.e., bent (fig. 181), we flick the back of the palm into the area described above (fig. 182).

DIM-MAK KNOCK-OUT POINTS

The following will describe in detail the most effective knock-out points using dim-mak strikes. These are the more accessible dim-mak points— those that are not as hidden and do not require one to have so

Figure 181

much training and accuracy to be able to make them work. They can be struck softly to cause a knockout. A harder strike, however, could cause death.

Each of the main knockout (KO) points has a training

Figure 182

method. These training methods extend to several areas of our martial arts training, providing the following:

- techniques to use against various attacks so that we can get to the points

- body movement to show us the best angles and evasive tactics to use when attacked

- the ability to "set up" the point when faced with different types of attacks

- the knowledge, at a subconscious level, of where the point is located on the attacker's body, so that we do not have to think about it when we are attacked

Dim-Mak Knockout Point No. 1

Stomach 9 is one of the most effective and dangerous points you can strike to cause knockout. If it is struck hard it will cause death, as the heart does not begin to beat again. A relatively easy way to get at this point when attacked is to use the back of your hand. If, for instance, my opponent attacks with a straight right, I should slam his forearm in an "away-from-me direction" to set up the point by rubbing the energy in the

Figure 183

Figure 184

opposite direction with my left palm (fig. 183). This action pushes his arm over to my right as the back of my right palm attacks to the side of his neck as in Figure 184. When using this weapon you can rest assured that you will get the point; you will not have to be that accurate. You do not have to use the set-up point, either. Just attacking this point with the back of the palm will be almost as effective.

A Training Method for Striking Dim-Mak KO Point No. 1

Your partner stands opposite you and throws a right hook punch to the left side of your head. You swivel on your heels, which will throw your left palm up and out to your left to make contact at the Pc 6 point on the inside of his wrist. Not only does the physical action strike inward, it also rubs along his inner forearm, away from his elbow and toward his wrist. This impedes the qi flow in the pericardium meridian. This is the set-up point.

As you are doing this, you thrust your right palm into St 9 (fig. 185).

Now your partner throws a right straight punch at your face.

You step to the left with your left foot to gain the best angle for your attack. Your left palm slams the outside of his forearm and slides upward from his wrist to his elbow, thus blocking his attack and, again, setting up Stomach 9 point. Your right palm now attacks to St 9 (fig. 186).

Your partner again throws a right hook, and you again strike to his Pc 6 point with your left palm but this time you strike his Stomach 9 on the other side of his neck using your right palm (fig. 187).

Figure 185

Figure 186

Figure 187

Another right straight punch causes you to slam his Pc 6 point again, down the inside of his forearm with your right palm. Notice the left palm moving up underneath your right palm to take over this blocking action (fig. 188). Now your right palm is free to attack his right St 9 point (fig. 189). You should now practice this routine on the reverse side.

Figure 188

Figure 189

Dim-Mak Knockout Point No. 2

This point has been used by boxers, mainly by accident, as it is relatively easy to get to and works even when the gloves are on. Figure 190 shows the location of the point, which is a special point located on no particular meridian. Striking this point back toward the back of the head blocks the signals from the central nervous system (CNS) from getting to the brain, causing the person to fall down. The technique for getting at this point can be the same as the last one if he attacks with, for instance, a straight right. The difference is that this time I must set up the point in the opposite direction, so I must slap his forearm in an upward direction

Figure 190

Figure 191

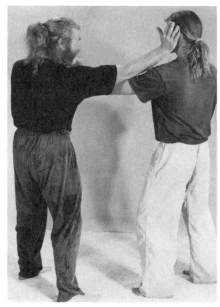

Figure 192

with my left palm as my right fist attacks to the point in the direction shown (fig. 191). Figure 192 shows another technique for getting at this point. He attacks with a straight left this time, so I slam his forearm back up his arm with my right palm. This sets up the point again, and then, without stopping, my right palm slams into the point. Here we have used one simple move to do both things—the setup and the dim-mak strike.

A Training Method for Striking Dim-Mak KO Point No. 2

Your partner attacks with a right straight punch to your face. You step to your left with your left foot, thus evading his strike. As you do this, your right fist can attack straight across his right arm to the point. Your right forearm also blocks his attack and slips up his arm to attack to the point (fig. 193).

He now throws a right hook punch. You swivel to your left and attack the inside of his forearm at Neigwan, while your right palm attacks to the point (fig. 194).

He again attacks with a right straight. Your right palm blocks his attack, and your left palm rises up underneath it to take over the block (fig. 195). Your right fist now attacks to the point (fig. 196).

He again attacks with a right straight. This time your left palm blocks on the outside of his forearm as your right thumb knuckle (the hand is held in a fist) attacks to Heart 3 on the inside of his forearm (fig. 197).

You now slap the outside of his right forearm with your left palm as your right fist attacks to the point (fig. 198).

You now practice the whole routine on the reverse side.

Figure 193

Figure 194

Figure 195

Figure 196

Figure 197

Figure 198

Dim-Mak Knockout Point No. 3

My previous book, *Dim-Mak: Death-Point Striking*, gave the locations of many of the most important dim-mak points. The locations of those that are not included in that book will be shown by way of diagrams here. Figure 199 shows Gall Bladder 19, which is just above Gall Bladder 20 (Gb 20) on the back of the head.

There are a number of different directions in which to attack the gall bladder points. To cause a knockout, we strike this point upward using the wrist-flicking method

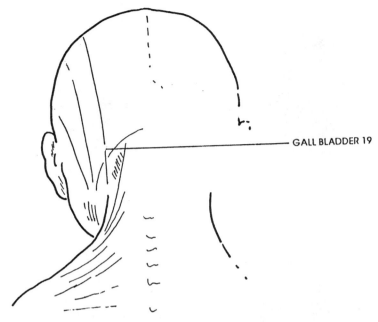

Figure 199

described earlier. The palm is loaded with yang energy, which is then released into the point by flexing the wrist backward. The point works better with a set-up point strike, as in the "willow tree" method from taiji, which is part of the training method for this point. Here we take his attack, perhaps a left straight, and slam it on the forearm toward us with the right palm, as in Figure 200. Notice that the left palm is cocked, ready to take over this action as in Figure 201. The right palm, which has moved upward as the left one has moved downward, now strikes in an upward manner to the point at the back of the head (fig. 202).

The back of the head is extremely sensitive, especially when struck upward. The skull is made to withstand downward blows but is not particularly strong when struck upward. There are so many important nerves at the

Figure 200

Figure 201

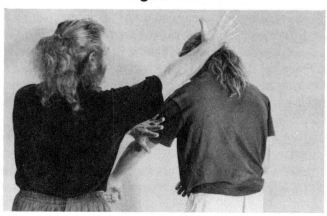

Figure 202

back of the skull that if you were to miss the dim-mak point, you would do damage anyway. So I urge you to use this area only if it is really necessary. Just a light tap on Gb 19 is sometimes sufficient to cause a knockout. Any harder a strike can cause great damage to the brain and cortex, resulting in death.

A Training Method for Striking Dim-Mak KO Point No. 3

Your partner attacks with a right straight. You block it with your right palm sliding down the inside of his forearm toward you. Your left palm has come underneath to take over the block (fig. 203). Your right hand is now free to strike using the back of the palm to St 9 point on the side of his neck (fig. 204).

Figure 203

Figure 204

Figure 205

Figure 206

Your right palm now takes his right forearm and moves it over to your right, which has the effect of turning his body (fig. 205). You can now strike the back of his head in an upward way using your left palm to Gb 19 (fig. 206).

Your partner now turns toward you and throws a left straight at your face. Your right palm slaps his arm, thus blocking it as your left palm rises above your right (fig. 207). The left palm now takes over this block, sliding down the outside of his arm and turning him again, this time to his right (fig. 208). Your right palm is now free to attack Gb 19 upward (fig. 209). This is the "willow tree" method. You

Figure 207

should now train the whole routine on the reverse side.

Figure 208

Figure 209

Dim-Mak Knockout Point No. 4

Conceptor Vessel 26 (Cv 26) is another extremely sensitive point, as striking it not only has the dim-mak effect, but results in a nerve-point knockout as well. This one can cause death if struck too hard. Located just under the nose where it meets the upper lip, it is struck upward into the depression. The following technique provides a way of gaining access to this point. He attacks

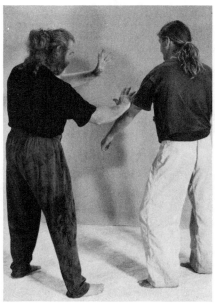

Figure 210

Figure 211

Figure 212

with, for instance, a left straight. I again slam his right forearm downward with my right palm as my left palm is getting ready to take over (fig. 210). My left palm now takes over by sliding down his forearm as my right palm slides up underneath so that I can strike to the point with the topside of my index finger, as in Figure 211. This point can be also struck with a number of different weapons, including the "tiger paw," as in Figure 212, wherein I take his right straight with my left palm and attack with my right tiger paw. Figure 213 shows the tiger paw fist.

Figure 213

A Training Method for Striking Dim-Mak KO Point No. 4

Your partner throws a straight left to your face. Your right palm slaps his forearm, sliding down it toward you (fig. 214).

As your left palm takes over the block, your right palm attacks to the point (fig. 215).

He attacks with a right hook. Your left palm attacks to Neigwan, on the inside of his right forearm, as your right palm attacks the point, this time with the small finger on top and the palm facing away from you (fig. 216).

He attacks with a left hook. You swivel and attack to Neigwan with your right palm as your left tiger paw fist attacks to the point (fig. 217).

You now do the whole routine on the reverse side.

Figure 214

Figure 215

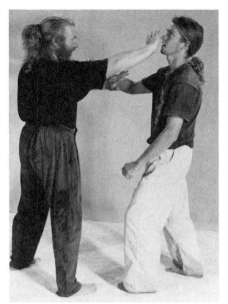

Figure 216

Figure 217

Dim-Mak Knockout Point No. 5

Yuyiao, as you may recall, is the Fish's Belly point and, again, is an extremely sensitive point due to its close vicinity to the eye. This point is located in the center of the eyebrow and directly above the pupil when looking straight ahead. Sometimes, as in the NS strike No. 4, we access this point directly from the outside, but in this case we will be accessing it from the inside, i.e., up into the eye socket. The tiger paw fist is the tool for this strike as well. This time we could attack the outside of the forearm just above the elbow joint at Colon 12 point with the back of the palm, as in Figure 218. Using the tiger's paw, the middle finger knuckle is then thrust up into the eye socket, as shown in Figure 219. Again, be very certain that the attack is serious enough to justify using this technique.

Figure 218

Figure 219

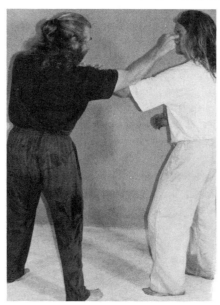

Figure 220

Figure 221

A Training Method for Striking Dim-Mak KO Point No. 5

Your partner attacks with a straight left. You slip your right fist along his forearm, thus blocking his attack and lining up his eye for the strike. Your right tiger paw fist attacks upward into his eye socket to the point (fig. 220).

He now attacks with a straight right. You block his forearm with your right palm, and your left palm comes up underneath to take over the block (fig. 221) as your right tiger paw fist attacks to the point (fig. 222).

He throws a left hook at your face, so you swivel, blocking his arm with your right palm to Neigwan. Your left reverse tiger paw fist attacks the point (fig. 223).

You now do the whole routine on the reverse side.

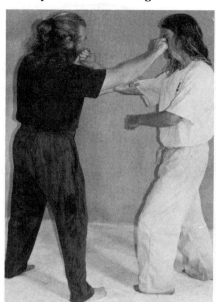

Figure 222

Figure 223

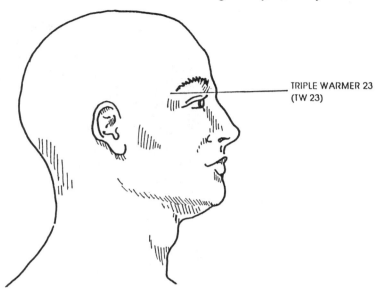

Figure 224

Figure 225

Dim-Mak Knockout Point No. 6

Triple Warmer 23 (Tw 23) point is a very useful knockout point that requires some physical ability to access. It is located just above both eyebrows in the depression at the outer corner (see fig. 224). We use the tiger paw fist in a downward way again, down the side of his face. We could access this point when he attacks with, for instance, a straight

167 ■

right, by slapping his right forearm back up his arm with the left palm and stepping to the left as the right tiger paw fist attacks downward onto Tw 23 (fig. 225).

A Training Method for Striking Dim-Mak KO Point No. 6

Your partner throws a straight left. You block by striking to the outside of his forearm and slipping along it so that it is moved to your left. Your right tiger paw fist attacks to the point in a downward way (fig. 226).

Figure 226

He attacks with a right hook, so you swivel to your left and slam his right Neigwan point with your left palm as your right palm slams the point downward using the heel of your right palm (fig. 227).

He attacks with a right straight. You step to your left and block his right forearm with your left palm as your right tiger paw fist slams downward onto

Figure 227

Figure 228

Figure 229

the point (fig. 228). This movement in particular requires some physical coordination and trains the brain and body to react together.

You swivel to your right to again block his left hook with your right palm to Neigwan as your left palm slams the point downward, as in Figure 229.

Next do the whole routine again on the reverse side.

The above points are by no means all of the knockout points on the human body. The death points will also work as knockout points, but many of them require so much pressure that a knockout will also do great physical damage. For instance, a strike to the ribs at Liver 13 will knock a person out but will also do great physical damage internally.

DIM-MAK CONTROLLING POINTS

There are many dim-mak points that, when used to a lesser degree of power, enable one to control the actions of an attacker. These are points I have given law enforcement people and bouncers (doormen) for when they require something better than clubbing a drunk who is a little out of order.

Dim-Mak Controlling Point No. 1

Triple Warmer 17 is also an extreme death point that drains the body of energy so badly that even CPR will not resuscitate the person. However, you can also strike this point with lighter pressure to cause the person to do what you wish him to, such as leave the room, sit down, and so on. Recall that its location is just behind the earlobe, a little below the hollow and in toward the jawbone. Pushing this point inward drains the lungs of energy and takes away a person's will to carry on an attack.

A technique that would make use of this point if, for instance, a person came at you with both arms, would be to first take both of your arms forward, thereby blocking his arms outward, as in Figure 230. Then you would use a light NS strike to the side of his jaw with your right palm as your left palm took up position at the right side of his face (fig. 231). With the longest finger of your left palm, you are now

Figure 230

Figure 231

Figure 232

able to press into Tw 17 to control him, as in Figure 232. If you find that this point does not work, you have simply missed it. Remember, it's a little further down than the ear hollow and must be pressed not straight up into the ear, but in toward the back of the jaw (toward you, if you are standing in front of the attacker).

Dim-Mak Controlling Point No. 2

An attack to the lungs in general tends to take away a person's will to fight. It does not have to be a lung point in particular, as other points also act upon the lungs.

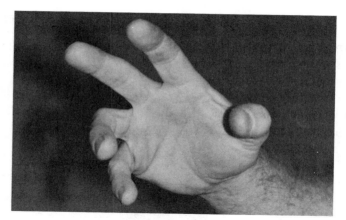

Figure 233

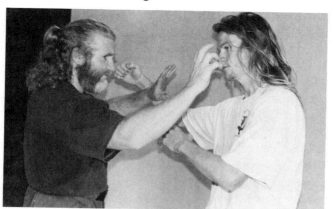

Figure 234

Figure 235

Stomach 12 is one such point. St 12 is on the top of the clavicle, a little more than halfway from the end of it at the neck end, in a straight line with the nipple. If it is used in combination with Stomach 11, the heart is also affected. The correct direction of the strike is straight down for both St 11 and St 12, which can be accessed by the following technique.

Recall how the palm must be held in order to gain the dim-mak claw (fig. 233). To attack St 11 and St 12, you could take your opponent's hook punch, as in Figure 234, then claw at the clavicle with the fingers of that hand, as in Figure 235. It is not necessary to know the exact location of the St 12 point, as one of your fingers will get it. However, if you aim to place your index finger as close to the neck as possible (into the clavicle notch, a small notch at the neck end of the clavicle), then your fingers should just fall into place. Now, with a downward pulling motion into the upper edge of the clavicle and slightly inside of it, the person will go down, not wishing to carry on.

Dim-Mak Controlling Point No. 3

I suppose any point that causes a human to do something he or she does not wish to do could be classified as a controlling point. However, the ones I am presenting here are those that cause a person to do what you want them to but not necessarily knock them out.

Lung 8 and Heart 5 are located on the inside of the wrist at the edges. All that one has to do to locate these points is grab the wrist and jerk downward. In fact, anything that attacks the wrist area will affect these two points. Remember, the heart and lungs control the will to fight, and if both are attacked, then it's "goodnight Irene," and we can pretty well do what we want with the attacker. Any good wristlock will work here, and I stress, a *good* wristlock—one that both turns the wrist inward and twists it. In bagwa we use these locks to great advantage. In fact, bagwa contains the most devastating locks ever invented, with as little as a quarter-inch being the buffer between broken and not broken. The effect of these wristlocks is a combination of pain and lost will to fight. It's not just pain that the person feels. If it were, then as any law enforcement person will tell you, it might not work on a drunken or drug-controlled person, who would not necessarily feel the pain. So the key is the combination of the pain and the controlling effect of these points. H 5 in particular drains energy from the heart; in fact, acupuncturists use it in medical cases where this drainage has to happen. Some acupuncturists go so far as to say that this point should not be used, as it has the potential to drain too much energy from the heart. In con-

Figure 236

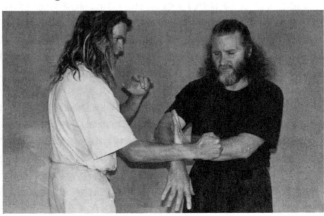

Figure 237

junction with Lu 8, then, it is used in the martial arts to do just that.

As I have always stated, no locking technique works in a realistic situation! Try to get a lock on some raving lunatic in the street, and you are in big trouble. However, if you can use some other technique to dampen the attacker's spirit before you get the lock on, it is a different story. This is the only way locks will work. The following technique uses H 5 and Lu 8 points in this way.

He might attack you low with his right fist. You should use a taiji technique to harm the inside of his forearm and also to attack to heart and lung points on the inside of his forearm (it doesn't matter which ones, as all lung and heart points will drain). This technique ensures that we attack to these points without requiring deathly accuracy. We slam his forearm using both of our hands. Both palms must be cocked and loaded with opposite energies (i.e., the right palm must begin as shown in Figure 236, and the left palm must be loaded as in the same photo). When the palms come together at the same time, slamming down onto his arm, they each release their respective energies by flicking in opposing ways. So, the right palm flicks backward and the left palm flicks downward as in Figure 237. This is not done with the arms and palms alone; the whole body must act here. It must be a fa-jing movement, where the body causes the palms and arms to move.

The next movements should be done as quickly as possible, but for the sake of practice, we do them slowly. To cause him to open his fist (if it is not open already), we slap the back of his right wrist violently with our left palm, as in Figure 238. Notice that the body angles have changed to accomplish this and the next moves. Notice also that by flexing, the right palm has loaded yin. Now pull his bent palm into your abdomen, locking it with your right palm bent backward, as in Figure 239. You are now able to let go with your left palm and are free to control him using only your body. Now you can use the left palm to attack further points if necessary.

Figure 238

Figure 239

Dim-Mak Controlling Point No. 4

An attack to Spleen 10 causes a person to fall down, once again, not from the pain but because of its action on the central nervous system.

Recall that this point is just above the knee on the inside center of the leg, just over that big bump in the hollow (see fig. 240). Because of its low position, we would not attack it using the hands unless we were on the ground grappling and could access it easily this way. Here, we use our feet to access the point. As he attacks by stepping in,

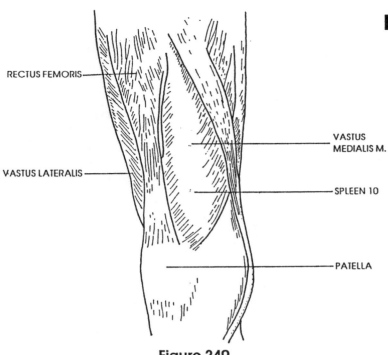

RECTUS FEMORIS

VASTUS LATERALIS

VASTUS MEDIALIS M.

SPLEEN 10

PATELLA

Figure 240

Figure 241

we should use the tip of our shoe to strike inward to the point as in Figure 241. Sometimes all that is needed is a push into the point to cause the person to fall down.

Sp 10 can also be useful, for instance, if the attacker has taken you down and is sitting on top of you as in wrestling (fig. 242). Here you should quickly move your hands into the correct position and squeeze very hard, pressing the thumb into the Sp 10 point. This will be enough to cause him to lose his concentration or to even jump off and allow you to counter.

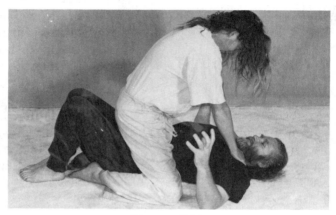

Figure 242

Dim-Mak Controlling Point No. 5

Bladder 57 (Bl 57) lies in the hollow created by the calf muscles, below the center of the popliteal crease, as shown in Figure 243. Again, you can access this point when the attacker has taken you to the ground and has perhaps been able to get you in a lock or is sitting on top of you. Grab this point and squeeze violently, and

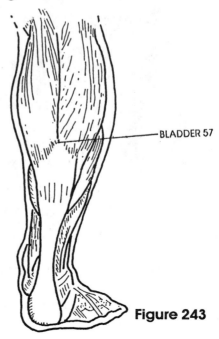

BLADDER 57

Figure 243

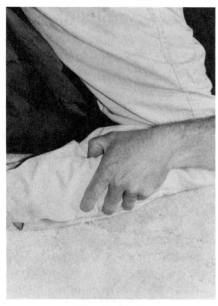

Figure 244

this will be enough shock to cause the attacker to let go, enabling you to kick him off and counter (see fig. 244).

Dim-Mak Controlling Point No. 6

Gall Bladder 40 (Gb 40) is located just forward of the ankle bone that sticks out on the outside, in the depression (or, to be more precise, anterior and inferior to the lateral malleolus, in the depression on the lateral side of the tendon of the extensor longus digi-

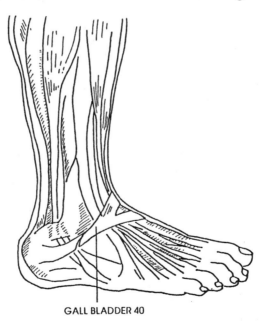

GALL BLADDER 40

Figure 245

torum). See Figure 245. When this point is pressed violently, the attacker will let go of his grip, allowing you to reattack or escape his hold. For instance, if you find yourself in the most unfortunate position depicted in Figure 246, you should find his ankle and attack it using your thumb, or thumb knuckle, as shown in Figure 247. And remember, all of the gall bladder points are knockout points as well, relying upon the action of the carotid sinus for the effect of the knockout (covered in great detail in my first book on dim-mak).

Figure 246

The above are the controlling points that I have found to work through experience. There are others, but they really require that you locate the point exactly, and as this is meant to be a practical book, I have only presented those you can be certain will work. If you wish for further detail, my video No. MTG55 covers all of the above.

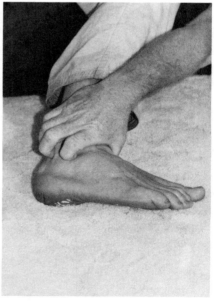

Figure 247

Chapter 7

Dim-Mak
and Knife Defense

The blinking of an eye and you're dead. That's all it takes, one second. You're alive, and the next second you're dead. This is what knife fighting is all about. People ask me to teach them about knife fighting, and I tell them that there is no such thing as knife fighting; there is only survival where knives are concerned. You cannot fight a knife. You might be able to give yourself the best chance against the human who is holding the knife, but to try to fight a knife is useless. So all we can ever hope to do is to survive.

I hear martial artists talking about knife fighting, about the correct technique, as if it is just another part of their training, something they do every day. Knives are death, and the way some talk, I wonder if they have ever really come up against someone who is trying to "get them," or if they have ever been threatened by some crazed person with a small glint of steel in their palm. I wonder this because of the techniques they tell us that we should use against such attackers.

"Techniques." This word immediately tells us that the

person talking knows nothing at all about survival ways against a knife. There are no techniques. You have no time to be thinking about techniques. You only have the time to react, and this "time" is the difference between life and death. No, there are no techniques, but there are ways of doing things that will give us the best possible chance of survival, which is, at its best, about 15 to 20 percent.

THINGS NOT TO DO

How many times have you been told that the best defense against a knifer is to run? Many times, I'll bet. I have, and I have heard others telling students that this is the best thing to do. When I give seminars to law enforcement people, I have them work an experiment. I become an attacker with a knife and I ask them, while I am standing away from them at varying distances, to turn and run as fast as they can and try to escape. No one thus far has been able to do so from a distance of less than 15 feet, with many not even being able to get away from a distance of 20 feet. And I am not a very fast runner. I am not able to get away when I am standing less than 15 feet away from an attacker.

The reason is simple and logical. As the defender, you must first turn to run, and if the knifer is on his toes, he will see this movement and immediately rush at you. Usually, the attacker is upon you before you have even taken the first few steps, and now you are in the most precarious position of having your back to him and not even being able to defend yourself.

I have three scars on my body from three different knife incidents. The first two represent my handling a knife attack the wrong way, while the third scar represents my almost getting it right!

The scar that runs from just below my kidneys to my lower right buttock represents my running away and having the attacker throw the knife. Luckily, he was not too good at this, and it is quite difficult to hit a target that is

Figure 248

Figure 249

moving either away from or toward you. The knife struck me with its cutting edge and not the point, slicing my lower back open. Luckily again was the fact that my attacker was not really intent upon doing real damage, as he fled at the sight of the knife actually striking me.

The second scar came when I tried to do what many people in the martial arts tell us to do—grab the arm that is holding the knife! There is not one streetfighter, not one thug, not one inmate of a maximum-security prison who will tell you to grab the arm that has the knife. At all costs, you try to keep as far away from that hand as possible, until the attacker has been stunned, downed, or knocked out. *Then* we should take the knife away; not when he is still fully active and full of aggression and at his strongest. In this case, I received a cut on my right arm about 6 inches long and to the bone. He simply withdrew the knife with much power—more power than I had to hold his arm—taking it over my arm as he withdrew it. Luckily again, he fled at the sight of my blood. Both of these incidents took place when I was a rock 'n' roller. To see how this can happen, look at Figure 248 for my attack and when the defender grabs my hand. In Figure 249, I withdraw the knife violently and cut his arm as I do it.

The last scar on my body is across my first three fingers of my left palm, from a cut that went to the bone. This is when I sort of got it right. Giving up a smaller part of my body for the sake of the whole, I was able to defeat this attacker and escape. This time, I went nowhere near the knife hand, but rather barged right in there and had my fingers sliced while my other hand was poking into his eyes. This worked very well.

So, we have things not to do: we do not try to run away, turning our backs on the attacker, unless we know that we are able to get to help before he gets us; we do not try to grab at the hand holding the knife; and we do not back off. I can show anyone that backing away from an attack is inviting disaster.

When someone attacks you, he expects certain things to happen. He has certain switches in his brain that tell him that things will happen a certain way. And when they do happen that way, he is happy. When, however, things do not go as he expects—in fact, the exact opposite—

Figure 250

Figure 251

Figure 252

then it is you who has the slight advantage. An attacker does not want you to come forward, for instance, slamming his knife arm so hard that it is knocked away violently, and then, while he is getting over this, to have fingers thrust into his eyes. There has to come a time when the attacker will be in range to attack you. He has to move in to you. This is the same for the empty-handed art.

He attacks you because he knows you are there. He would not attack you if he knew that you weren't going to be there! So do not be there. We do not move backward. He is going to get us sooner or later if we continue to be the attackee.

We do not do the old "X" block. I still see this silly block being taught, and I can demonstrate how silly it really is. This type of block has come about because people teach others about knife attacks in dojos—safe and sound, no real attacks, not even simulated attacks. Note what happens when a person is attacked with a downward thrust, as in Figure 250. If the attack is for real, it will burst right through the "X" block and end up in your chest or face, as in Figure 251. Or you will have your wrists sliced, as in Figure 252.

Nor should we try to barge right in there and slam him in the face. See what happens in Figure 253 when he tries to slam me in the

Figure 253

face. He is stuck in the ribs for his trouble. I still hear people saying things like "Oh yeah, I'd just slam him in the face. I don't need any of this dim-mak stuff," etc. Now, any law enforcement officer knows that there are many cases where a slam in the face is useless. The attacker is crazed—drugged, drunk, or both, and pain just does not work. Here, I can explain and show that there are points that work on the human body that do not cause pain; they cause human phenomena that cannot be defended against—physiological things such as neurological shutdown, where the nervous system simply gives up. Usually, the people who make these statements are good ring fighters and use the martial arts for sport, having no idea of the reality of the streets.

Lastly, you should definitely not try to get some kind of lock or hold on the person with the knife, at least not while he is still fully powerful. Locks and holds are fine, just as long as you have taken care of business first. Strike him at dim-mak points or, at the least, slam him in the face to stun him, then get the lock on.

THINGS TO DO

I have worked on ways that will give us the best possible chance of survival—not much chance, but the best—against a knife attack. I am realistic enough and have had all the experience I wish to have with knives to know that there is not one system that has the exact answer, least of all mine, but here I will give what I believe to be the best "way" of dealing with knife attack.

First, get mad. Fear will often help here. It will cause you to change into something else. You must do this in order to be just as mad, or even madder, than the attacker. Do not make a perfect martial arts yell, but rather, scream! This screaming will help get your adrenaline right up there. Scream as you attack him; it helps. Open your eyes as wide as possible and stretch your fingers

Figure 254

wide and tight. This will bring extreme yang energy into your brain and body, helping with the transformation from human to animal, which is what you must become in order to survive.

Then you remember the three words *evade, bump,* and *strike*. Remember, do not actually grab the attacking arm, but rather, bump or slam it violently so that you not only hurt it but move it

187

out of the way for that split second, enabling you to attack. For instance, the attack could be a straight lunge-type attack. You could use the "hinge" arm (the forearm is bent and hinges downward) to damage his attacking forearm and get it out of the way. This is both "evade" and "bump," as shown in Figure 254.

Figure 255

Notice how my right arm was thrown up into the air automatically, ready to strike. This I did not have to think about. Doing the "hinge" attack to his forearm gave me the body movement to cause my right palm to be thrown upward. I struck his forearm violently—so violently that it caused my own body to shake. (This is fa-jing, or explosive energy.) This put the rest of my body in a state of rebound, ready to attack his eyes or any other important dim-mak points, such as Stomach 9 or the vagus nerve in the neck, which controls the "state" that the heart is in (i.e., pumping or in arrest) and reverses it. I automatically turned my waist to "bump" his forearm, thus "evading" by bumping his arm out of the way. Now a split second later (and still part of the initial movement), my right fingers are thrust into his eye sockets. Don't just poke his eyes. Do a proper job and dig down into the sockets, as in Figure 255. In this way you are also attacking to Stomach 1 (St 1) points, located on the lower part of the eye socket bone in a straight line with the pupil (when a person is looking straight ahead) and just inside the eye socket. If a finger is poked into the eye and pulled down, the point will be found. Such an attack will cause extreme nausea because of the action on the liver. It will also cause him to "look inside," literally, as his eyes will be forced to turn inward. Extreme? Sure, but what is happening to you is extreme; one split second and you're dead! So yes, extreme.

The most important part here is that you do not try to control the attacker's arm, leaving your own arm in contact with his. You are not trying to "push" his arm away, but rather bump it away, so that you have only minimal contact for that split second. And in the time when his arm is moving away, you attack to points.

Evade, bump, and strike is a way that works with all types of knife attack, and I advise you to experiment with this, as there are endless possibilities. In time you will begin to know where and when the attack will be coming from by having your partner attack from all different angles with a wide variety of strikes. You're not just playing, though. You must get as near to real aggression as possible with this, with your partner really trying to get you, fast and hard. However, he must of course have that

Figure 256

immediate control so that if something does go wrong, as it will, he is able to stop just before he strikes you. Even rubber knives can give nasty cuts.

The same applies to, for instance, the hook type of attack. This time, you evade by moving in and turning to your left as he attacks with his right hand. Both of your hands slam his inner forearm so hard that his arm is thrust away, as in Figure 256. Notice where I have struck his forearm. My right palm is striking right into the crease of his elbow, while my left palm is striking to Neigwan. The Neigwan point will drain energy from his body, while the strike to the inner elbow is a nerve point strike that will not only take his arm out but also cause extreme nervous damage to the whole body.

Now, again, without stopping and using the energy generated from the initial strike,

Figure 257

turn the body and strike across his neck with both palms. You are bound to hit something here! There are just so many vital points in the neck—dim-mak, nerve, and physiological points—that any strike such as this will be fatal (fig. 257).

IMPORTANT POINTS

Never become complacent about your knife defense. Never think that you have the answers. Always work in as realistic a way as possible, having your partner attack with animal aggression. If you are able to grab his hand, then he isn't doing it right. Only use the above as a guide. Experiment and work out your own best method, using the "way," rather than the technique. Never turn your back. Move in at the right time; do not back away. Become the animal aggressor—don't give him a chance to attack, attack him first. Be prepared to give up a smaller portion of your body in order to survive. If you *are* a law enforcement officer and you are within 15 feet of the attacker, do not attempt to take out your gun. He will get you before you have had the time to take off the safety catch. If you judge that this person is not really intent upon killing you, try to talk calmly and without any threat to him of aggression, but always on the ready for danger. Take a really good look around you at your surroundings, not taking your eyes off him. Do not stare at him, but rather use your peripheral vision to "look around." Let him know that you aren't there to hurt him. And, most importantly, if you are not a law enforcement officer, do not be in that situation in the first place. Law enforcement officers have to put their lives on the line every day and find themselves in these situations all the time. There's nothing much they can do about it.

Point Power

I n this chapter I will cover the main revival points, as well as the emergency points. The revival points, including the heart starters and the lung starters, are those that will revive someone who has either been knocked out or badly mashed up—if he can be revived! The emergency points are those we use when all else fails, when someone is so badly knocked out that even CPR will not work. The body has been so badly drained of energy that it does not have the power to start the heart again, like a car with a battery so flat that nothing works. However, we do have an emergency system, and if we know how to get at it to pump some stored qi into the body, this is usually enough to get the heart to start if we then follow it with CPR.

REVIVAL AND EMERGENCY POINTS

The Heart Starter

In my last book I covered the heart starter briefly, and as this section would not be complete without it, I will discuss it here in more detail.

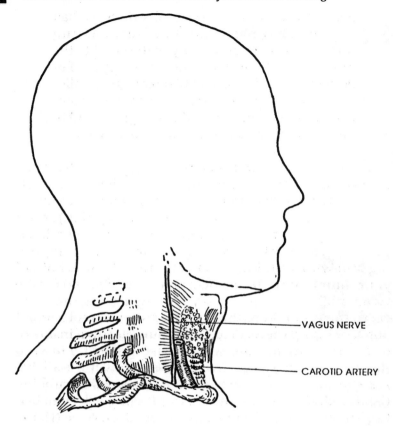

Figure 258

The vagus nerve is the most important part of this procedure. We are able to get at this nerve by simply striking into the neck, or if we wish to use it for healing (heart starting), we can locate it under the clavicle notch, as in Figure 258.

The vagus nerve is sometimes referred to as the "pneumogastric" in older texts. According to *Gray's Anatomy* (1991 edition):

> The pneumogastric, or vagus, one of the three divisions of the "eight pair" [of cranial

nerves], has a more extensive distribution than any of the other cranial nerves, passing through the neck and cavity of the chest to the upper part of the abdomen. It is composed of both motor and sensitive filaments. It supplies the organs of voice and respiration with motor and sensitive fibers; and the pharynx, esophagus, stomach, and heart with motor influence.

Suppose your opponent or sparring partner has been knocked out, and you find that his heart has not restarted. (The heart stops momentarily or falters when one is struck in either the vagus nerve or at St 9 point.) Don't panic! That's the main criterion here—try to stay calm. If you are by yourself, sit him up in front of you, supporting him with your knee, as in Figure 259. Place both of your thumbs into the clavicle notch (see fig. 260 for the location). If you simply run your finger along the clavicle to the end where the neck is, you will feel a small notch or bump there. Place both thumbs down inside of this notch and into the neck, pressing slightly inward (toward the neck) and down (fig. 261). Pressing is all that is needed: however, some people also say that rubbing the thumbs backward and forward will work even better. I have only had to use this procedure once (thank God), and it worked with pressure alone. You press for about five seconds and then, supporting the person (it is better if there are two of you, so that the other person can support him while you perform the next procedure), you strike either one side of the backbone (if you are by yourself) or both sides simultaneously (if you have someone to support him) in an arc over Bladder 15 and 16 (Bl 15 and 16) points, as shown in Figure 262. (It's as if you are rubbing your right palm counterclockwise beginning at the top of his scapular and going around it to end up at the lower side of his trunk.) The left palm does the opposite. Bladder 15 is located 1.5 cun lateral to the inferior border of the fifth spinous process of the fifth thoracic vertebra. Bladder 16 is the same distance laterally to the sixth vertebra. The strike should not be too weak; it should be powerful enough to move the patient forward as you strike, but not so powerful as to knock him over! If someone does it to you while you are awake, you should feel your lungs quiver so that you feel like coughing. This should

Figure 259

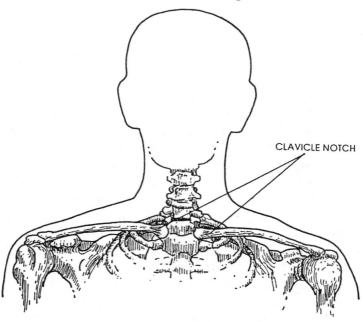

CLAVICLE NOTCH

Figure 260

Figure 261

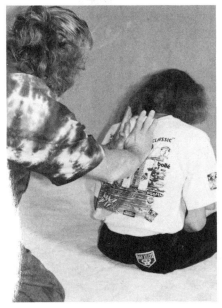

Figure 262

be enough to start the heart beating again. If not, do it again, and if this does not work, then you should try some of the following procedures to release the stored qi from the kidneys so that the heart has some energy to get started.

All of us have a well of qi in our kidneys, stored for use in an emergency. But it won't come out automatically; it has to be coaxed out and into the system if the person is badly hurt and unconscious or clinically dead (i.e., his heart has stopped beating but the brain is still okay).

Kidney 1 (The Bubbling Well)

Kidney 1 (K 1) point is located on the underside of the foot (the only dim-mak point on the sole of the foot), just between the two mounts of the large toe and the one next to it (fig. 263). This point is one of the major emergency points on the body. When a person has been so badly knocked out that the heart has stopped beating, this point will cause the stored qi to come back into the body and allow the heart to again beat using CPR. The effectiveness of this point depends upon the basic health of the recipient to begin with. If he or she is healthy, young, and not overweight, then there should be an ample supply of stored qi in the kidneys. You can be older and have an abundant supply of qi, but Westerners tend to deplete their supply of qi as they grow older from failing to do the correct things in life (see

Chapter 10: The Warrior's Way of Health). It is also possible to build up that stored qi again by changing life-styles.

Kidney 1 point is usually made to bleed by sticking something into it and breaking the skin! But then, if the person is dead, I don't think he or she will mind you doing this. If you do not have a sharp

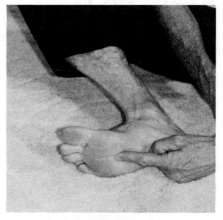

Figure 263

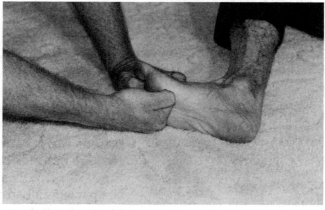

Figure 264

object, then a good, solid punch up into the point using one knuckle will do (fig. 264). This point is used in acupuncture to cure emergency states such as coma. It is also used for dizziness, fever, lethargy, and eye problems. It has a strong action on the head and the sensory preceptors and is a major revival point because it releases stored qi through the cheng point connections and through direct action upon the kidneys. "Cheng" means to complete, and in acupuncture it denotes the extremity points, such as Colon 1 (Co 1), at the tip of the index finger just to the outside of the fingernail at its root nearest the thumb. Kidney 1 can also be used with Co 1. By using another extremity point along with K 1, we are able to cause the cheng point connections to work even better at directing this stored qi to where it has to go.

Gall Bladder 20 (Wind Pond)

Gall Bladder 20 (Gb 20) is an overall revival point, used not so much for releasing stored qi into the system, but for when someone has been knocked out but the heart has not

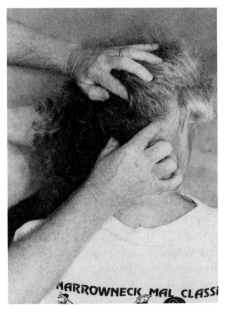

Figure 265

stopped beating. It is located in the depression that lies between the sternocleidomastoideus and the upper border of the trapezius, on a level with the mastoid process and just below the edge of the occipital (in other words, just under that big lump on both sides of the lower edge of the skull). We use the thumb and forefinger to squeeze and press upward into the skull (if the person were not knocked out, he would "feel it"). This brings qi into the head, clearing the mind and strengthening the vision (fig. 265).

Colon 1 (Merchant of Yang)

Colon 1 is an emergency point and is used in cases of coma. Again, it is usually bled; however, a good sharp squeeze at each side of the index finger at the base of the nail will do the trick. At a lower level, we can use this point when we are in danger or afraid or need a little bit extra in a hurry. You should grab either side of the nail and squeeze sharply. It is also good for clearing the mind when one is feeling a bit scattered.

Lung 11 (Young Merchant)

Lung 11 (Lu 11) is situated on the lateral side (outside) of the thumb, 1 *fen* (one-tenth of an inch) superior to the base of the nail. Squeeze the thumb sharply at both sides of the thumbnail. This point is a "wood cheng" point (an extremity point that is assigned the elemental aspect of wood in Chinese medicine, meaning it is used in emergencies to revive) and is used to boost the "wei qi" (the qi that flows around the outside of the body to protect) when one is attacked externally. When squeezed, Lu 11 releases wei qi to the surface of the body. This point will help in lowering the shock value, at least, when one has been struck or cut externally.

Pericardium 9 (Middle Assault)

This point is also a cheng or extremity point, with the healing aspect of wood in Chinese medicine. Its location is on the thumb side of the middle finger, 1 fen posterior and lateral to the angle of the base of the nail. It is usually bled for emergency treatments such as coma or heart stoppage. It is also good for when you have been struck in the ribs and feel that you are going down, as well as in cases of heat exhaustion or heat stroke for eliminating heat. Just grab the tip of the middle finger and squeeze it sharply on both sides.

Heart 9 (Small Assault)

Heart 9 (H 9) is located 1 fen lateral and posterior to the lateral angle of the root of the little fingernail (on the inside of the little finger, close to the base of the nail). Again, it is a wood and cheng point. It strengthens the yin or yang qi of the heart and is used as a revival point in coma, as it brings extra qi into the channel system and directs it to the *zhang*, or "heart control consciousness."

Spleen 1 (Hidden White)

Spleen 1 (Sp 1), another wood and cheng point, is on the outer edge of the big toenail, 1 fen superior and medial to the medial angle of the root of the big toe. It is used for the calming of the mind and for menstrual problems associated with irregularity. It is bled for manic-depressive states and is used as an emergency point for shock and coma. Spleen 1 is good for controlling bleeding, especially in the gastrointestinal tract and the uterus. It is included here for its value in controlling extreme shock because of its input of qi into the upper, middle, and lower heaters. This point connects "heaven with man," helping to promote a tranquil, dream-free sleep. Squeeze sharply at both sides of the big toe. This point must not be used in pregnancy or in the case of diabetes because of its action on the pancreas.

Spleen 3 (Supreme Whiteness)

Spleen 3 (Sp 3) is located on the medial side of the foot, posterior and inferior to the first metatarso-phalangeal joint (big toe joint), just superior to the tendon of the abductor hallucis muscle (fig. 266). This one can be called a revival point because it will revive a person who is down because of "aftershock" (i.e., someone who has perhaps been in a fight and is okay for awhile but suddenly faints because of shock). Apply pressure with the thumb straight inward to the foot.

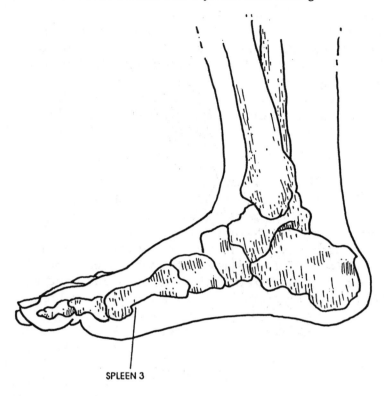

SPLEEN 3

Figure 266

Heart 7 (Doorway to the Spirit)

Heart 7 (H 7) is located on the left side of the wrist (when you are looking at your right palm), just up the forearm a tad from the wrist crease in a hollow (fig. 267). It is included here because it is the major point for calming the whole spirit and has emotional control over the whole system. Often it is used in conjunction with Heart 3, on the inside of the elbow crease, for severe emotional problems and insomnia. Stroke this point for about 1 inch using mild pressure in the direction that is from the wrist crease to the elbow.

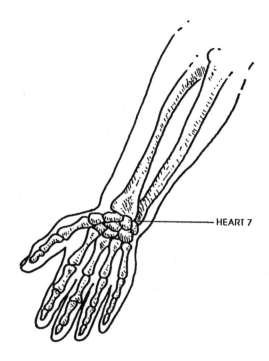

HEART 7

Figure 267

Bladder 67 (Arrival of Yin)
This point, located on the outside of the little toe just above the nail base, is used when someone is "out of it," dizzy, or the mind is not in control. Squeeze the tip of the little toe sharply to clear the mind and strengthen the eyes.

These are the major points used in dim-mak at a revival or healing level. All of them, of course, are used as dim-mak strikes as well. The difference is the level of pressure used and what is in the "doer's" mind at the time—whether he or she wishes to heal or do damage.

While we can use these points for healing by summoning stored qi in the kidneys, it is also possible to use them in the same way for self-defense when we are in a dangerous situation. We summon this stored qi through the use of the "C" back and the reptilian brain. Then the qi simply comes out and helps us in the situation, giving us that extra something over pure physical ability alone, like a turbo-boost. This is where the stories of so-called fantastic feats of strength come from. In such cases, a person simply has access to his or her stored qi. It is quite difficult for someone who has had little or no training to actually bring this qi forward, but there *have* been cases where people have lifted cars off of loved ones after accidents, and so on. This is rare, however.

Note that once you have used up your stored qi, it takes around six hours for it to be replaced, so if you are making use of it in a life-or-death situation, you had better be sure that your technique is good so that you are able to down the attacker in the first few seconds.

Ways To Bring Out the Qi

The eyes say it all. If you look into the eyes of someone who is making use of the stored qi, you see something different than just normal-looking eyes. It's as if something is coming out of the eyes. This is not just a widening of the eyes, as this is a purely physical thing. Rather, the thought that brings in the turbo-boost should make the eyes do something. Look at Figure 268. I have tried to bring up the qi so that the eyes change. It's an internal thought that causes certain physical

Figure 268

and chemical changes to happen in the body, as if something is rising from your lower back and into your upper back to just under your skull. Again, this is exactly what happens to an animal when it senses danger. The back arches. The whole body is relaxed, but internally alert and strong. The weight is centered on one foot, in the middle of that foot. Your arms should feel like there is an electric current running through them. This is because there is one.

In periods of danger, we, too, can make use of this physiological phenomenon that occurs in animals through all of the years of training required to bring the qi out. This training must be of the so-called internal type, for instance, taiji or bagwa. But beware! Not all internal schools are the same. There are not many that teach real internality. So you could spend the next 30 years training very hard and at the end of it have nothing!

The best exercise for making use of the stored qi is the post, which is presented in the first chapter of this book.

Once you have done the initial work, this stored qi will be there for use naturally, and you won't have to do anything to bring it out. At the precise moment of danger, you will find that it is over—someone is lying on the ground, and you do not know what it was that you did.

This is true internal power. It cannot be brought out for demonstration in a seminar, nor on the television to help people perform amazing feats of strength and power just to satisfy their egos or show off, etc. Something unexpected happens at the right time, and it never lets you down. However, you must do all of the right things in order for this to happen. This does not mean just the physical training. It means that you must look at everything you do, all of the areas that use qi. You must look at the "warrior's way" of eating (the food you eat), the sex you have and the way you do it, the thoughts you think, and the very air you breathe and the water you drink. These are all factors in how much stored qi you will have to save you in an emergency. (I cover the above areas in Chapter 10: "The Warrior's Way of Health.")

THE ORIGINAL TAIJI FORM

Doing the taiji form correctly causes us to have the "C" back. It is not possible otherwise, simply because there are certain physical criteria that must be met in order to cause the qi to rise up the back. An onlooker who does not know exactly what it is he is looking for and knows nothing about the reptilian brain or the ways to get it will not see any difference between a normal human way of standing and the way one must stand to get the reptile brain. In Figure 269, you see me just standing there, being a human being. But what do you see in Figure 270? You might see that the back is slightly more rounded, you might even notice a different look in the eyes, but do you see what the legs are doing?

The legs are being forced outward by the action of the hips opening. But it's not just that the legs are being pushed outward; you can do that by forcing your knees out. Rather, it is like there is a pneumatic jack inside of your hips, forc-

ing them outward, which, in turn, pushes your legs out slightly. But it's from the hips and not the knees. As we move, that slight internal tension will relax, and then it will activate again. This is called "opening and closing," or yin and yang. This occurs all the way through the original Yang-style taiji form. I don't mean the rubbish that is being put forward as the original Yang style by most people, but that which

Figure 269

Figure 270

was invented by Yang Lu-ch'an.

This opening of the hips causes us to have the "C" back and allows us to implement the most important classic of "raising the back," i.e., causing the qi to rise up the back from the tan-tien and end just under the skull at the points called Gall Bladder 20. Now, we are ready to be attacked! We are in a reptile brain mode.

Qigong

I n my first book on dim-mak, I introduced basic qigong. In this chapter, I will take that a step further. For those who don't have that first book, a brief introduction to qigong follows.

To some people the word "qigong" means magical, mystical feats of superhuman strength, with old men bending iron bars in their nostrils, breaking granite blocks with their heads, etc. To others it means a way of healing certain diseases, otherwise incurable by Western medicine. To others it's a new exercise fad.

Many external stylists are now turning their attention back to their roots, using the Chinese systems, namely qigong, to enhance their arts. These people are finding that they are only able to take their art to a certain high level until their bodies just won't do any more. That's when they turn to qigong.

Some karate stylists have tried to invent their own qigong systems, and some have been successful. But others have taken their qigong to the same absolute tension that their katas have to be taken to, and so have failed at gaining that something extra from their arts.

So what is it? Well, it's not a way of becoming Superman, so those of you who are considering taking up qigong to make you invincible, forget it. However, if you want to learn how to use what you have more economically and with much more natural power—and, in the process, become extremely *well*—then qigong is for you. You will not be able to perform such feats as the old sword in the neck trick, as seen in Figure 271. This is a trick of leverage where the attacker actually handles the spear so that the power is going upward onto the chin and not into the neck.

Figure 271

You don't have to be studying a Chinese style to use qigong. All that is required, especially for the "hard" stylists, is that you completely open up to a new way of doing things which will, in the beginning, be totally alien to what you have been taught.

Qigong allows your natural internal energy, or electricity, to flow freely to all parts of the body.

I will say here that, contrary to some belief, the internal energy *does* flow to the head; if it didn't, we'd all die. Some people have written articles telling of the dangers of qigong, madness supposedly being one. Of course, if a person is on the knife edge already, then it would be inadvisable to take up qigong unless under the watchful eye of an experienced teacher or doctor. There are twelve main and eight extra acupuncture meridians throughout everyone's body. These are the channels for the flow of qi, and there *are* some in your head! Neither will you go mad from the practice of qigong if the qi gets into your brain, for God's sake! It has to. As we grow older and we become more tense (usually as a result of twentieth-century living), these channels are gradually blocked to the flow of qi until they become completely blocked and we die. The doctors attribute this to some disease that has attacked us from the out-side. More to the point, the qi has slowed down, thus stopping our natural self-healing mechanism from working correctly.

In the martial arts we use qigong not only to make us well, but also to give us something else in the way of power and speed. Obviously, if our muscles are so tense from overdoing the weight training, we are unable to use them correctly. We sometimes use our muscle groups adversely so that different groups work against each other. This muscular tension then stops the bones, tendons, and sinews from working correctly, and the whole body becomes rigid, usually to the point of putting bones out of place permanently, so that we are only able to use, for instance, the triceps when throwing a punch, rather than using the whole body to whip the punch out at great speed and power. You can have big muscles, but they must not become so tight that they are always active when they shouldn't be.

There are about 2,000 different types of qigong, which are grouped into the following three main areas:

SELF-HEALING

This is where we are able to use certain postures with certain deep breathing techniques to allow our own self-healing mechanism to spring back to life, sending life-giving qi to all parts of the body via the meridians.

MEDICAL

This is where we are able to heal others who are sick by putting our own qi into their acupuncture points to assist their own healing systems. This is quite advanced, however, and takes years to master. We use certain breathing techniques with certain yin and yang palm postures to send a continuous flow of energy into the point. An acupuncture point is only a point on the body where there is a least amount of resistance to electrical energy. A seasoned practitioner is able to rub his palms gently over the patient's body until there is a slight "dragging" or sticking feeling where the acupuncture point that needs healing is situated. Only the point that needs the healing will be sticky, though, and this is where qigong is far more advanced than acupuncture. Nowadays there are electronic implements that sense where these low resistances are on the skin.

Qigong is also used as a total healing method. That is, the "doctor" of qigong is able to use the qigong stances not only to heal, but also to diagnose any problems.

He or she does this firstly on a large scale, placing the disease into one large area of the body and determining whether it is a "yin deficient" or a "yang deficient" disease. The way the doctor establishes this (on a very basic level) is by taking note of the position of the palms after some minutes of the patient practicing his her own qigong stance. (The positions of all of the limbs is also taken into account, but for this book I will only deal with the more simple palm positions.) If, for instance, the right palm has fallen to a lower level than the left palm, this indicates that there is a yang deficiency on the right side of the body. (The position of the other limbs helps to establish if upper or lower body is affected.)

To further pinpoint the problem, the doctor places the patient into a series of other postures, including some of the taiji postures, to find out which ones cause pain or are much more difficult than any of the others. If, for instance, the posture of "brush knee twist step" causes some pain around the chest area and is grossly difficult (more so than normal for a beginner) to perform, this would indicate a heart problem of the yang-deficient variety. Further examination, taking into consideration the tongue, face, and skin condition, would further confirm the diagnosis. The qigong doctor then determines how to heal the ailment. He may decide to use acupuncture to heal the immediate effect of the pain and then use some qigong postures to put some yang energy into the heart. He may also practice his own qigong—for 20 minutes if it's a minor ailment or, for a more serious disease, for 10 days, eating only fruit for that time. He will then place his palms around the affected area or over the relevant acupuncture points and put his own yang energy into these points to further help the cure.

There is a point on the palm called Laogung, or Pericardium 8. This is said to be the point whereby the qi is sent from one body into another. If you close your fist and see where the longest finger points to, then this is the point to which I am referring.

Figure 272

The doctor will also decide upon a certain qigong posture to cure the disease. This will sometimes be a posture from the taiji form and is usually the exact same one that was used to diagnose the disease.

The posture can be a static one used with certain breathing techniques—either cleansing or tonic, prenatal or postnatal, reverse or natural. It can also be a moving posture.

For instance, to heal something relating to the joints, the "single whip" posture (fig. 272) may be used as a static posture. The same posture is used to heal the digestive tract; however, the difference is that in this case one moves from the posture of "press forward" (fig. 273) to "sit back ready" (fig. 274) and then into "single whip." This is the way it goes in the taiji kata or form. It is then held for a few minutes and repeated.

If you are practicing taiji using the correct breathing technique for each movement, then you are already practicing qigong. There are some postures that are simpler and therefore easier to use than the taiji postures, and these were invented for this very reason.

MARTIAL ARTS

In the martial arts

Figure 273

Figure 274

we use certain postures with breathing techniques to cause a flow of qi to particular groups of muscles to help them work more effectively with much more power. However, everyone must first of all begin with the basic qigong for good overall health.

Firstly, we must build up some more of this stuff called qi. So we have a stance called "three circle standing qigong."

PRACTICAL

I covered the basic qigong stance and how to do it in my earlier book. There are four different qigong exercises that will enable you to take the basic qigong to a more advanced level. The four qigong exercises are done together *before* you begin your martial arts training or your basic qigong training. This will completely balance out the amounts of yin and yang energy in your body.

Figure 275

Opening the Gates

This qigong (the first of the four) will help in the opening of the "gates." These gates lie up your spine and down the front of your body and must be opened before you can begin any internal training. This exercise is noncumulative. Therefore, when you finish, you will stop before beginning the next exercise.

Stand as for basic qigong: feet parallel, arms hanging loosely at your sides but not "dead," shoulders relaxed and rounded naturally, as in Figure 275. The tongue is on the hard palate. You will use a natural breath for this exercise. Natural breathing involves allowing the lungs to do what they want to naturally. They expand (thus expanding the lower abdomen) upon inhalation and contract (thus contracting the lower abdomen) upon exhalation.

Figure 276

The chest does not rise as you breathe in; the lower abdomen moves out. As you do this, turn both palms over and lift upward (fig. 276). Your hands will now rotate and move outward and begin to go down. As this happens, your knees will also go outward, and you will lower your body by bending your knees (fig. 277). You are now breathing out. When you get to a position where you can no longer keep your back

Figure 277

Figure 278

Figure 279

vertical, your hands scoop inward and your knees do likewise, so that you are knock-kneed. Your tongue now drops to touch the lower palate, and you begin to breathe inward (fig. 278). Your hands will again turn upward and lift as you begin to straighten your legs (fig. 279). You are now breathing in. Next, your hands turn downward again and move outward. Your knees follow. As your hands and knees come back into a normal position, you breathe out, lifting your tongue back up to the upper palate, and you sink your knees again (fig. 280).

This is a completed exercise. You now stand up to finish. You must perform this exercise three times. Remember, as you breathe out with the tongue on the upper palate, you must breathe out of your mouth. When you breathe in, it is through the nose.

Gathering the Qi

You begin this exercise about one minute after the opening of the gates. Stand as for the basic qigong. You breathe in and out through the nose this time, and the tongue stays on the upper palate. Begin with an out breath as you push outward with both palms, as if cutting away from yourself in an arc downward. As you do this, your weight will rock back onto your heels (fig. 281). You now turn your palms toward you as they reach upper chest height, and this is the end of the exhalation (fig. 282). As you draw your palms in toward you, as if taking something into your mouth, your body rocks forward onto the balls of your feet and you breathe in (fig. 283).

You now push your palms outward and down again, the same way that you began this exercise, and breathe out, pushing yourself back onto

Figure 280

Figure 281

Figure 282

Figure 283

your heels (fig. 284). This is the beginning of another round. Your palms have done a complete circle, moving up when away from the body and down when close to the body. You repeat this exercise/round 36 times (this is a positive number in Taoist thought). However, as you continue, you will feel a tightening sensation, like you are unable to move your arms in such large circles. So the circling of the palms becomes smaller and smaller so that by the twentieth round you are hardly moving them. In fact, to an onlooker, you are not moving at all. Internally, you are still doing that same round, but externally there is hardly any movement.

Packing the Qi

The gathering exercise is cumulative, which means you do not stop after the thirty-sixth time. Rather, as you bring your palms down on the thirty-sixth time, instead of continuing with the circling, you will join your thumb, index finger, and longest finger so that the index fingers and thumbs form a diamond shape (fig. 285). The diamond shape is right over the tan-tien, about 3 inches below the navel.

Figure 284

Notice that the elbows are not held inward but outward. This places natural pressure inward onto the three fingers. You must relax your arms so that you feel the natural inward pressure. If someone, for instance, pulled your palms apart, they would feel a spring. If they let them go, the palms and arms would spring back. You must not force your fingers together; just allow the natural spring tension to happen. You simply stand in this position, breathing naturally, deeply through your nose.

After 10 minutes,

Figure 285

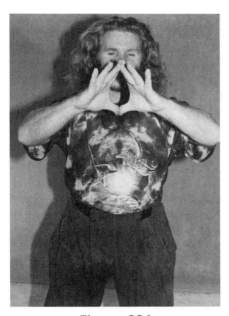

Figure 286

you should move your arms upward *without losing the natural tension.* The final position allows you to look through the diamond shape formed by the forefingers and thumbs. The tops of the index fingers are in line with the upper tan-tien (between the eyebrows), as in Figure 286.

Closing the Gates

This is done so that all the good you have just accomplished will not be lost. You must close the gates. This is, again, cumulative, so you go right into it from the packing. As you allow your fingers to come apart, you turn your palms upward and allow them to move apart and downward. Your tongue is still on the hard palate. You breathe in (fig. 287). Bring your palms up and over so that the *fingers only* (not the thumbs) touch. Place your tongue down onto the lower palate the moment the fingers touch. As you push the fingers together so that the mounts will meet, you breathe out from your mouth (fig. 288). It is important that you do not allow the palms to touch. Only the fingers must touch to the mounts. This will be quite difficult to achieve, as you are trying to get a 90-degree angle between your fingers and your palms. The ease with which you can do this gives you an indication of how much gunk there is in your body, physical or mental. Easier and there is not too much, but very difficult and there is much. This is also a cleansing qigong and can be done while fasting to eliminate toxins. Now you bring your fingers apart again, and as soon as the tips of the fingers part, return your tongue to the upper palate as you breathe in. Bring your palms down and out slightly (fig. 289). The finishing of this posture involves a fajing movement. You must clap your palms together as your entire body shakes, and exhale making some sound like "hah!" (fig. 290). Walk around slowly for about five minutes to come out of it completely.

Figure 287

You will find that this series of qigong exercises will be quite powerful, and many strange things will happen. Everyone is different. Some shake violently, some feel like they are floating, while others don't remember a thing afterward.

BREATHING

There are four main breathing techniques that we must use with

Figure 288

Figure 289

Figure 290

qigong. Here I will only deal with the first method, as it takes 3 years of practice before going on to each successive technique. The four techniques are natural breath, reverse breath, prenatal breath and tortoise breath.

Natural Breath

This breathing technique is as it sounds, but for most of us, breathing has become unnatural, so we must first of all learn how to breathe naturally again. Look at a small child before any "living stress" has entered its mind. The child breathes with the lower part of the abdomen, where the bulk of the lungs are. Most adults tend to breathe only with the upper portion of the lungs, drawing in the abdomen and sticking out the chest.

If you simply relax your whole upper body, shoulders, chest, etc., then there is only one way that you can breathe. Stick out your gut on the in breath and allow it to collapse on the out breath, like a balloon filling up and deflating. Don't force your breath, just allow your motor reactions to work for you. Breathe in and out when you want to, and only breathe in until your lungs are full; don't try to get more air in there.

This is the natural way of qigong breathing, and, when combined with the stances, it makes for a most potent healing/martial aid.

MARTIAL STANCES

I can't, of course, cover all of the qigong stances here, so I will cover some of the more useful ones for the martial arts.

Once you have trained in the healing qigong for at least three months and you are able to hold the stance for at least 20 minutes, then you should go on to the more strenuous martial qigong stances.

Holding the Baby

The normal healing qigong takes an equal amount of qi to the upper and lower body, while the martial qigong is able to take different amounts of qi to different parts of the body, depending upon which parts need it most. Most martial artists need much support from their legs, so

Figure 291

we begin with the legs.

The "holding the baby" qigong looks just like holding a baby (fig. 291). You are now standing with most of your weight on either leg (right leg in the photo) with the palms held so that the elbows are over the corresponding knees. This puts the leading palm out further than the rear palm. Still, the one line of skin between thumb and forefinger is held, and the breathing is the same. The gaze must be out over your "dragon mouth point" (Colon 4, or Co 4, at the base of the thumb where the second finger joins the palm). The inner palm is placed 7 *tsung* from the other wrist. (In Chinese measurement, from the wrist to the elbow is 12 tsung.) The body is held in the same manner as for "three circle standing" qigong, only now you must notice "the three things."

It is important to

Figure 292

Figure 293

take note of three areas in this stance, otherwise you could do yourself some damage—your muscles could collapse! First, there will be a piercing pain, like a red-hot needle going into your standing thigh. Next, you will feel this pain dissipate all over your thigh, and finally, you will begin to shake. This is the time to change to the other leg. Don't just stop and change legs, though. Slowly shift your weight onto your left leg (other leg) and bring your right palm (inner palm) under your left (fig. 292). Take a step with your right foot so you end up in the opposite position from the one you started in (fig. 293).

You now repeat the three things and then change back to the other leg. You will notice that each time you change, you are able to hold the posture longer. You should be able to get it up to about three minutes, but not all at once. Make sure you give each leg the same amount of time.

A more advanced, "one-legged" qigong is the same as the previous one, but with the whole weight on one leg. The leg that is resting over the other knee should be totally supported by that knee; i.e., you shouldn't have to hold your foot up there. It just rests (fig. 294).

Squeezing Qigong

This is an advanced qigong that takes most of the qi into the forearms and finally into the whole skeletal structure to give us *zheng gu*, or bones of the tiger. This is where we cause the qi to change state, like placing a cauldron of water over a fire, thus causing the water to change

Figure 294

Figure 295

Figure 296

to steam. The qi changes to jing (the form it must take to be used by the body, just as water must be turned to steam in order to drive a steam train) and travels to the marrow of the bones, where it condenses and turns into fat. Thus the bones become tightly packed with marrow, making them very strong (thus the old Chinese saying "iron wrapped in cotton" with reference to a taiji person's arms).

The lower body is the same as for "three circle" qigong (fig. 295). The arms are held out from the body and hang slightly downward. On the in breath, the palms open outward slightly with a yin aspect, i.e., they are not flexed. As you do this, you imagine that there is a vise squeezing in on all parts of your palms, squeezing the bones from all sides. As you exhale, you squeeze your palms slightly inward using a yang, or

227

slightly flexed palm (fig. 296). You now imagine that the vise is relaxing its hold, and the force is now going out of your palms from all sides. The movement of the palms is only about 6 inches to begin with, but as the qigong progresses, the movement decreases until there is only internal movement. There should come a feeling of resistance between the palms, to the point that it becomes a physical resistance and you really do feel as if your palms are being sucked together as you squeeze outward and pushed out when you squeeze inward.

Upon finishing this stance, you should lower your palms slowly and breathe in. Then clap the palms together with some force as you breathe out, also with some force. This should feel like a shock wave, and there should be a sensation of something rushing from the back of your skull down to an area about 3 inches below your navel, but on the backbone side.

Two-Person Qigong

The above qigong method can be practiced with two people. The two people stand opposite each other with their lower bodies in the normal "three circle" qigong stance. The palms are touching, one person on the outside with the other on the inside (fig. 297). As one person pushes his palms inward, the other person with his palms on

Figure 297

Figure 298

the inside provides a slight resistance. The person pushing breathes out, while the other breathes in. Now the person with the palms on the inside pushes out and breathes out while the one with the palms on the outside breathes in and resists slightly.

There is a more complicated two-person qigong. Now each person has a palm on the inside and a palm on the outside (fig. 298). As one person pushes in with one palm, the other resists with the corresponding palm and pushes with the other palm while his partner resists.

On the "coming in" movement, both partners breathe out, while on the out movement they breathe in.

With continued practice of qigong, everyone will experience great benefits to health as well as to their own martial art.

CHINESE SEASONAL EXERCISES

Definite chemical and energy changes happen to the human body at each change of season. In order to take full advantage of these changes, the Chinese have, over the centuries, developed a series of exercises to utilize the great amount of new energy.

Most people have experienced the initial changes in

energy that a new season brings, even if it is on the very basic level of just feeling great at the beginning of spring or feeling a bit dull when winter sets in. But to feel all of the other changes, and to use these changes for positive action, even the autumn and winter energies, we must have a way of seeking out the minute energy changes and making use of them to help us to learn and grow, physically as well as spiritually.

To do this we have to distinguish between the seasons on a qi level, so that we can perform the correct exercises to enhance whatever energy the particular season brings and eliminate the bad energies, pushing forward the good. For instance, at the beginning of autumn and spring, there are very powerful "middle yin" and "middle yang" energies, respectively. These two energies usually bring good feelings, with spring being a yang time, for building, and autumn a yin time for internal work (i.e., building of the spirit or character, reflection, etc.). But there is the danger, especially in the autumn, of allowing this yin energy to take us into melancholy, or cause us to "wait until spring again" to start doing things. There is also the danger at the beginning of spring to allow this yang energy to cause too much excitement and happiness, which will be detrimental later on, as everything must have its opposite.

Both yin and yang energies are equally powerful and equally good or bad, depending upon what we make for ourselves during these periods. And usually what we make of this energy early on is a measure of what will come. So it's important to get whatever we can out of these changes early, so that the whole season will be enhanced.

The Chinese exercises for the seasonal changes are designed to smooth out the great energy changes so that there will not be so much of a "downer" when the opposite energy arrives and vise versa, and also to utilize the good energy so that the rest of that season will be full of growth.

Times for the Exercises

It is not necessary to watch the calendar and take the exact date on which we are told spring will begin as the starting date, although this is a good ruler as to an approximate time for the change of seasons. Some people are sensitive enough to feel when the changes occur without the use of a calendar. Others will feel something happening but will not be too sure. For this reason, we practice these exercises for five days either side of the calendar date of the start of the new season, morning and evening, for about 20 minutes each day. The time of day is also important, as we must have a balance of the energies that these exercises bring. The absolute correct times are when the day emulates the season. For instance, summer is represented by noon, while winter is represented by midnight, these being extreme yang and extreme yin. Spring is represented by dawn while autumn is represented by dusk, being coming out of yin into yang and coming out of yang into yin, respectively. But none of us usually have the time to work out at these times, as we must go to work. So we choose the times that will give us the most balance: morning, yin into yang and evening, yang into yin (spring and autumn, figuratively).

The Exercises

Just before the beginning of spring, we begin the following series of exercises to enhance the middle-yang energy of spring. These exercises have a balance of yin and yang, swinging slightly toward the yin to coincide with the season's slightly more yang energy. We also begin with the yin exercise.

Standing relaxed with the weight evenly distributed, cross your palms in front of you, facing you, as you breathe in through your nose, deeply but not forced, right down to your lower abdomen. Be sure not to expand your chest; relax it and allow your lower abdomen to expand (diaphragm breathing). As you do this, lift your right foot so that the sole points to the knee. Your left knee has bent slightly so that the knee comes over your left toes (fig. 299).

Turn both palms over, away from you but still touching at the wrists, and push both palms out away from you so that they will make about a 100-degree angle as you straighten your left, or standing, leg. Breathe out through your mouth. This is a cleansing breath designed to get rid of any bad energy from the winter (fig. 300). Now, as you swing your right foot out away from your body, breathe in through your nose (fig. 301). Make a slight clockwise circle with your right foot and bring it back to its starting point as you lower your body, bending your left knee again and exhaling through your mouth. Take your foot to the ground and relax your arms to your sides and wait about 10 seconds before beginning the whole routine on the opposite side, swinging the left foot out and making a coun-

Figure 299

Figure 300

Figure 301

Figure 302

terclockwise circle. Repeat this exercise five times on each side. Then take a rest.

You must perform the whole routine as slowly as possible with great flow of movement—no stops or starts.

The balancing exercise, or yang set, is performed after you have rested for about five minutes following the previous exercise. Start as before with your feet evenly balanced. Raise both palms to about shoulder height. The right one in this case will be in front of the other with the palms pointing outward (fig. 302). Breathe in through your nose as you turn your waist to your right, thus taking your palms over diagonally (at a 45-degree angle) to your right, as in Figure 303. Notice that the palms have turned to your right, ready to strike something. Now, lift your right foot and move it over to your

233

left-hand side. The right foot will now make an arc from left to right as your palms travel from right to left, meeting in the middle to slap your right foot on its instep (fig. 304). Breathe out through your mouth. Do not stand up on your toes as you strike. To finish, the palms carry on over to your left in that same arc as your foot, in the same arc over to your right and down to the ground (fig. 305). You finish by bringing your palms over your knees and changing your weight onto your right foot (fig. 306). You should repeat this exercise on the left side. Do it five times on each side and then have a rest.

Go back and repeat the first exercise and then the second. You should repeat these exercises three times, resting between each set, but be sure to finish with the yin set (the first one) so that you have actually done

Figure 303

Figure 304

Figure 305

more of the yin exercise. Do not overdo it in the beginning. You might like to only try one set of each until your ligaments become a little more stretched. If you are in bad shape, of course, only try these exercises in moderation to make sure that you do not tear anything. As with anything, progress gradually up to the highest level.

Figure 306

For the Beginning of Summer

These exercises are yin in nature and offset any tendency to over-indulge in the summer energy.

Stand with your feet flat and about double-shoulder-width apart. The breathing is done all through the nose for summer. Bend forward at the waist slightly and tuck your right palm in toward your waist. Do not breathe as you do this (fig. 307). Breathe in as you swing your right palm first to your right and then out to your left and begin to straighten your torso (fig. 308). Keep breathing in, and stop as you bring your right palm over your head (fig. 309). Breathe out as you bend forward again, cutting your right palm down in a counterclockwise circle back to the beginning position.

During this exercise you should be able to place an object onto

Figure 307

Figure 308

Figure 309

your palm and not have it fall off. The palm remains upright at all times. Repeat this seven times on the right side and go straight into seven times on the left side. Have a rest and then repeat the whole procedure two more times on each side. Take it easy if you are not well or in bad shape; perhaps only twice on each side is enough. This exercise should be performed slowly with deep, regular breathing. You should feel as if you have done something, but not to the point where your heart rate increases greatly.

The Autumn Exercise

Autumn is another "middle energy" time, so again, we have two exercises to perform.

For the spring exercise we began with the yin part, so in autumn we begin and end with the yang part, so that we have more of the yang. We breathe in through the mouth and out through the nose. This is a tonic breath to fortify us for the coming winter energy. It's a bit difficult if you have a cold, but try anyway.

Figure 310

Stand with your feet turned in slightly. Raise your palms to about shoulder height in a slight counter-clockwise arc out to your right side as you begin to breathe in (fig. 310). Turn your waist to your left, which carries both of your palms over to your left, turning them in the same direction (fig. 311). Bring your palms inward to your chest while holding your breath, and then thrust them out to your right

Figure 311

Figure 312

Figure 313

side as you breathe out with a fa-jing energy explosion. The palms thrust out to the side, as if striking something, as you lower your weight slightly (fig. 312). Repeat this three times, then do it three times on the other side. Take a rest and go into the yin part of this routine.

Stand with your feet parallel and place your right palm on your right hip. Your left palm is hanging at your side. Breathe in as you swing your left palm out to your left side and bring it up and over your head (fig. 313). Bend at your waist to your right as the circle continues (fig. 314). Drop down with both arms dangling as you slowly breathe out (fig. 315). Place your left palm onto your left hip and swing your right palm out to your right as you stand up (fig. 316). Now repeat this procedure on the other side. Each time you bend

239

forward, dropping your palms, you place the opposite palm on your hip and the opposite side begins. Perform this exercise three times on both sides, then repeat the yang exercise once to finish and rest. Unlike the yang side of this exercise, this part is performed with no explosive movements, all flowing.

Figure 314

Figure 315

Figure 316

Figure 317

The Winter Exercise

The winter exercise has to be yang in nature to offset the extreme yin energy of winter.

The breathing is done through the mouth, provided that the air is not too cold to cause throat troubles on the in breath. If it is too cold, perhaps place a scarf around your mouth to warm the air as it goes in.

Stand with your left foot forward and your palms turned

241

inward (fig. 317). While breathing in, lift your left foot off the ground and leap into the air as your palms lift out to both sides (fig. 318). Your left foot stomps down where your right foot was (it comes back a step), as your palms begin to fold in. You breathe out as your right foot stomps down onto the ground where your left foot was (it takes a step forward) and your arms cross. (fig. 319). With the last bit of air in your lungs, explode it out as you punch with your left fist (fig. 320) and then pull it back. From here you turn your palms up and repeat the whole exercise on the other side. Only perform this exercise twice on both sides to begin with, as it brings great yang energy into play. You might like to leave out the leap into the air, preferring to step through it until you are able to perform the

Figure 318

Figure 319

Figure 320

leap. Either method will produce the desired effect.

This brings us to the end of the Chinese seasonal exercises. I see nothing wrong with using these routines all through each of the relevant seasons. But do not use the wrong exercise for the wrong season, as it can have an adverse effect.

The Warrior's Way of Health

Your body is a road map of your life. Every wrinkle, every bulge or crater tells the story of your life. Depending upon what we do to ourselves throughout our lives, we can either be simply an older version of the beautiful young person that we were, or we can be someone who bears no resemblance whatsoever to that young person.

An older person is not ugly, or rather, a person should not become ugly as he or she grows old. The beautiful young person is capable of also becoming a beautiful older person. However, there are certain rules that one must follow in order for that to happen. Smoking, drinking alcohol, eating rubbish, and having bad thoughts and sexual habits are all ways to become the unrecognizable person in older age. On the other hand, not smoking, not drinking, eating the correct food and having good thoughts and sexual habits are all ways of becoming the beautiful old person by increasing your reserve of qi for when you become older. It is also possible, however, to regain qi by doing the correct things, even after one has led a "not so qi-orientated" life.

The amount of qi we have into older age is dependent upon the good things that we did with our bodies and minds when we were young. And if we have more qi, then we are still beautiful, even when quite old. This is because "beauty" is really only skin-deep. Real beauty goes much further inside.

You can, for instance, see the most technically beautiful young person, and although you know that she or he is beautiful because that's what you have been conditioned to believe, deep down you really may not see that person as being beautiful. And he or she may not really attract you, apart from a few animalistic urges! Meanwhile, you might see someone who is not perhaps so *technically* beautiful, but who has an inner beauty and an abundance of qi and really attracts you—moreso than the technically beautiful person. But that attraction is something more than just thinking of having sex! It is an inner attraction that all living things have for each other.

All living things—whether a tree, a dog, a snake, or a human being—attract each other. And it's an attraction based on the mutual experience of simply being here, alive. But by doing all the wrong things, a product primarily of twentieth-century living, we lessen that attraction because we become less alive. Our magnetism is slowly depleted. This is especially true for drug and alcohol users. Their qi is slowly taken inside to try and heal the damage being done, leaving very little for attraction.

We communicate with each other not so much with physical words and movement, but by internal intercourse, when our energies combine and communicate. The more energy, the more communication. I do workshops all around the world, and the first thing I do when I enter a room of 50 or more "strangers" is to extend my own energy to literally surround the whole group. This tells me immediately what each person is all about and causes all of their energies to combine, which has the effect of bonding the whole group for the workshop. They not only communicate with me, but also with each other, which allows them to take in what I am teaching more easily.

When I was young, I was a rock 'n' roll star with a number of hit records to my name. There were many beautiful young girls who flocked around the band and so forth. Nowadays, I look at some of those same people, and in many cases I am unable to recognize them. Some, however, are still extremely beautiful and still have that attraction. These are the ones who led healthier life-styles as they grew up and, in particular, did not smoke or drink.

Me? Well, I think I started on the right path too late! Too many women and too much drugs and rock 'n' roll in my early years, I'm afraid. But I try. Nowadays, both my wife and I are getting older (me more so than she), but we still love each other even so, and I still see her as an extremely beautiful woman, because real beauty is simply ageless. Your inner self does not have to become old; like the moon, it stays beautiful forever.

The "warrior" is not just a person who is able to fight. Fighting is only one-tenth of being a warrior. The warrior knows about health and how to heal. The most important area of a warrior's trade is knowing about the use of energy—how to use it more efficiently and how to use it to change his circumstances, including his health and well-being. He also knows how to use this energy to help others to change.

How does one know when he is healthy when he has not experienced real health? It's a bit like the fish in the fishbowl who does not know anything about the outside world. We just hack the life we have, thinking that all of those little or large illnesses are a natural part of living. The M.D. becomes our best friend.

Take a logical look at the human race compared to, for instance, a small bird or insect, or any animal out in the wild. Then you will see that we human beings are the weakest of all the animals—great brains, but weak of body. We martial artists have pictures taken training in cold waterfalls or doing push-ups in freezing streams, etc.

We call this strong. Then we go to our comfortable homes and switch on the TV. We are weak. The last real human warriors stopped being so around the turn of the century. (I'm talking here of the native races of North America, Australia, South America, and so on. They were the real warriors.)

But it need not be like this, and it is relatively simple to change what we have become. With a bit of "energy management" and correct living habits, we can slow down or sometimes even reverse the gradual decline of our human bodies.

Do not mistake "fitness" for good health. I have seen the fittest of people die young of heart attack; this is not good health. On the other hand, one can be super-healthy and not be able to run a mile. Fitness and health do not necessarily go hand in hand. It's better to be fit and healthy, but if you cannot manage the two, then better to be healthy than just fit.

FOOD

We begin with the food we eat. I have seen some miraculous things happen simply as a result of changing the diet. Over the years, through personal experience and research, I have developed theories about eating that have often contradicted what the "authorities" were currently saying about nutrition. My ideas about food are my own, and they may not necessarily coincide with modern scientific thought. But this I know for a fact: there is nothing surer than "you *are* what you eat." Eat live food and you will be alive. Eat dead food, and you will be dead (earlier than normal). Eat second-rate food (that which has come from an animal) and that is what you will be.

We human beings need to eat what was given to us from the beginning (of the human race). Just think, if you were the first human being on Earth and you were hungry, what would you eat? Would you look at a cow and think that it would be a good idea to eat it? Would you look at some grain and think it looked nice, smelled nice? No. You would be attracted to something that attracted your senses. Like an orange or apple or banana. We were given these foods (fruits and vegetables) by whatever created us.

As we eat more and more junk, the body begins to slow down, to grind to a halt. It becomes clogged up. This affects the mind, and we become moody and depressed, so we eat more food as a crutch. So the cycle continues until we die prematurely. Our loved ones blame the illness on some microbe or virus, some disease that attacked us from outside, when all the time it was our own doing— our weakness of body—that invited the disease in.

Dogs eat meat; humans do not. It sounds radical, but it's true. The dog has a relatively short intestinal tract. Its food is in and out quickly, so the meat does not have a chance to turn putrid inside. Humans have a relatively long intestinal tract, and if we eat meat, it has time to become putrid, full of poisons. If, however, we eat fruit, we are able to get it in and out quickly enough (because it is easier to digest) so that it does not putrefy. (Fruit also takes longer to become putrid.) The extra strain on the whole system from having to spend many more hours and much more energy on digesting meat shows in the end. We are left with not enough energy for the whole being, and so we become ill.

It would take a whole book to tell about the horrors of milk products, so I will give the briefest of information about this twentieth-century nightmare. (For more on my ideas on eating, however, you might want to read my book entitled *Food for Spirit*.)

Milk is the scourge of the Western world. More diseases can be attributed to the huge intake of milk products than to any other food. I have reams of information from the Central Emek Hospital in Israel (one of the leading authorities on milk-related diseases), which contain actual accounts of people being cured of disease (asthma being one of these, along with bone diseases) by simply being taken off all milk products.

The dairy corporations of the world are so strong that they are able to suppress any real information regarding the dangers of milk intake. Some years back, *Healthview* magazine ran an article by Dr. William A. Ellis, whose findings were somewhat astounding. "There is overwhelming evidence," he said, "that milk and milk products are harmful to many people, both adults and infants. Milk is a contributing factor in constipation, chronic fatigue, arthritis, headaches, muscle cramps, obesity, allergies and heart problems. Also, many suffer from undiagnosed lactose intolerance."

Ellis said that it was not necessarily cholesterol in milk that was the problem, but rather "an enzyme in cow's milk called xanthine oxidase [XO]. XO causes heart problems by attacking the heart's arteries."

According to Dr. Kurt A. Oster, Chief of Cardiology at Park City Hospital in Bridgeport, Connecticut, "From 1971 to 1974, we studied 75 patients with angina pectoris and atherosclerosis. All the patients were taken off milk and given folic acid (a B vitamin) and ascorbic acid (Vitamin C), both of which combat the action of XO. The results were dramatic. Chest pains decreased, symptoms lessened, and each one of those patients is doing great today. . . . The problem is even more severe with cheese."

Dr. Kurt Esselbacher, Chairman of the Department of Medicine of the Harvard Medical School, stated his theory about the enzyme XO as follows: "The problem of XO in milk seems to lie exclusively in homogenized milk [all processed milk today]. When milk that has not been homogenized is consumed, the body excretes the XO. However, when milk is homogenized, the particles are broken down so finely that the XO is absorbed into the bloodstream. From there it attacks the heart and artery tissues."

Infants make a substance called lactase, which is able to break down milk into its two main sugars so that it can be digested. At about the age of 2, we humans stop making this stuff and are unable to digest mother's milk thereafter; hence, the natural weaning process which is seen in all animals. Some races have evolved such that they continue to make lactase, but it is my belief that this is a product of the body trying to compensate for wrong eating habits. We, as adults, are not supposed to drink milk. It is for babies.

According to a friend of mine who is a chemical scientist, "Phytannic acid ($C_2O\ H_4O\ O_2$) is a fatty acid derived from milk and is indigestible because of its chemical structure. The phytannic acid accumulates in the body tissues, causing serious neurological problems."

In any case, who wants to eat something that comes from the inside of a cow?!

ENERGY MANAGEMENT

If there is anything that could be classified as magical in life, then this is it: how we can manage our energy systems, causing that energy to be redirected to other areas to do work for us.

There are three main users of energy in the body. The greatest of these is procreation, or "sex," as some like to call it. Obviously, the most important human function is to create other humans. We have to use the most pure energy we have to go into the making of another human being. No, don't put the book down now; I'm not going to tell you to give it up! Just try not to ejaculate every time. I know it's a challenge, but this is part of the magic.

The Chinese texts tell us that we should "do it" twice in summer and once in winter! This is because ejaculation is a huge user of qi. On a base level, this is the same advice that is given to boxers. They are told not to have sex while training because it has been learned over the years that sex gives them weak legs. And this is true. It may be okay when we are young and have much yang energy, but as we grow older, we lose too much energy if we ejaculate too often. Sex is okay, and plenty of it—it's the ejaculation part that depletes the qi. (This only applies to men, by the way; climax does not deplete a women's qi supply.) It's a difficult thing, but once they have done it (i.e., held the sperm), men feel great afterward, like a boost of energy has gone into their bodies. There is, in fact, in Chinese medicine, a way of using sex as a healing method by using the "higher" or "superior" ejaculation (i.e., stopping the sperm from coming out at the crucial moment). The ancient Chinese texts tell us that one superior ejaculation per "session" will heal the liver, two will heal the heart, and so on until we get to ten. And then we see God! Well, actually, they tell us that we are on the way to becoming "gods," or enlightened people.

The next biggest user of energy is digestion. The less we use in this area the better. So it stands to reason that the easiest food to digest is the best food to eat. Sure, cooking makes food easier to digest, but is also takes much of the goodness out of the food, so that we have to eat more of it to gain the same building blocks that we would if we ate it raw.

Bodily movement, thought, and physical things, collectively, are the third biggest user of energy.

Into our energy management comes the yin and yang theory. Most of the ancient races knew about this. For instance, Roman Nose, the great warrior of the Southern Cheyenne who became famous around the 1860s for his great battles with the U.S. Army, knew about yin and yang (not so much the words yin and yang, but the actual use of them). Roman Nose would "take in some yin" by fasting for four days and lying out in the hot sun on a raft on the lake, taking neither water nor food. He would also cut his legs and arms before going into battle. This was his way of investing in loss. He would then ride his horse along a line of American soldiers who fired upon him relentlessly, and he would not be struck. His horse was shot down once, but he was not hurt. On one occasion, however, he did not have enough time to do his ceremony of "investing in loss," and he was killed! Here lies the magic.

The laws of nature tell us that for every up there *must* be a down, and for every down there *must* be an up. If we give up certain things (like food or sex) for awhile, we gain more energy for our inner minds to be able to change things for us. I have experienced this many, many times, and it has never let me down. When things are going not so well for you, you should "fast, think, and wait." Things will change after you have invested in loss, because, as sure as winter, there will be a gain to balance out that loss. So fasting is a part of the warrior's way of health, the use of energy to help us in our daily lives.

The Fast

There have been many ideas on fasting, but when it all comes down to it, fasting simply means to not eat or take any nutrients. There is no such thing as a "juice fast," because if you are drinking juice, you are still taking nourishment. There is no danger in fasting, provided that you do it sensibly and not for too long in the beginning. The danger lies in coming off the fast and what we eat then.

When we fast, the body gets rid off much of the gunk that has been stored in our fat cells over the years. (This is sometimes called cellulite, those ugly fat lumps that appear in women in particular on the triceps or the thighs.) All of the toxins that are ingested, and which are not eliminated by the kidneys or liver, etc., are readily stored in those fat cells. When we fast, that poison is drawn out of the cells. So we end up with a whole lot of poison in the system that has to be got rid of.

Drinking pure water during and after the fast is important, as it helps to prevent dehydration as well as dilute and flush out some of the poisons. Equally as important is the food we eat after the fast in helping to eliminate the poison, taking it back out via the kidneys and liver. But the danger is that if too much of this poison is being taken through the system at once, then we may kill ourselves!

The human body must be kept slightly on the alkaline side, rather than the acidic side, to maintain good health. There are acid-binding and acid-forming foods. Those that are acid-binding (alkaline in nature when broken down in the digestive system) are good for us because they attract the poison and take it out. Those that are acid-forming are not good for us, as they form poison that is then stored. So when we come off the fast, eating some really acid-binding foods, such as grapes, will result in much poison being eliminated at one time, and this is where we might get into trouble.

When first attempting to fast, we must eat foods afterward that are sort of in-between in terms of their acid-binding properties, like bananas or apples. These will only bind to a small amount of the poison. We must steer clear of grapes, dates, sultanas, figs, and olives, as these are highly acid-binding. After undergoing a number of fasts, one is relatively clean inside and can take the acid-binding foods after the fast, as there is not as much poison to be eliminated by this time.

When I was young, I was allergic to the type of gas dentists used in those days. Every time I went to the dentist and had to have gas, I would be ill for days afterward, starting with vomiting all the way home in the bus! I remember this quite well. Later, as an adult, I began my first fasts. Being the proverbial "over the top" type of person, I did a 15-day fast to start with. After this fast, I drank a liter of grape juice and ate around 2 pounds of grapes! I thought that I was going to die, so my wife called a doctor. We found out that I was being poisoned by that very gas that I was allergic to as a boy! Yes, it was all still stored in my body and only came out when I fasted.

So this is not the way to go. We must take it easy when fasting. Good things to eat after a short fast (around two to four days) would be apples and bananas and perhaps some apple juice. (Do not eat oranges or other citrus foods or juice.) Do this for the first day, followed by taking a potassium broth made up of the peelings of root vegetables, such as potatoes, beets, carrots, etc. This will get your system back to normal again after the fast.

You will find that you will be ill on the first day or two of the fast, and then it will get better. This has to do with the elimination process removing the poisons from your body. You will be up one day and down the next. If you suffer a slight headache, take some warm pure water with a teaspoon of honey dissolved in it. This will usually work in taking away the headache.

My students all know when I have been fasting, as they are knocked around more than usual in training! You will find that you have much more energy and become more robust after the fast.

Nowadays, my family and I eat only "food." We define food as being that which grows in the ground and can be consumed directly without cooking or processing—mainly fruits and vegetables, very few grains, and no rice.

All fruit is alkaline when broken down in the digestive tract. Even citrus foods turn alkaline when digested. Things like meat and dairy products do not. Grains are for cattle. Cattle have the teeth to grind them up; we must first of all boil or grind them in order to digest them. Rice makes a great woodworking glue because it has so much mucus, and this is what it eventually does to your insides. It's okay for the Chinese or Indians—they have iron stomachs, which evolved over many thousands of years of eating these grains (although one of the things that Gandhi tried to do in India was to get the people off rice and onto wheat grains; he failed).

The warrior needs to eat things that will not only make him strong of body, but also strong of mind and character. The thing most people ask when they are learning about fruit eating is, "Will I become weak and skinny?" I ask them to look at me. Am I skinny and weak? Look at a gorilla—is he skinny and weak? One of the strongest animals in the jungle eats leaves (and the occasional banana)!

A word of warning, however. Depending upon what you have been eating most of your life, your system will react more or less to a drastic change in eating habits. If you have been brought up on hamburgers and fries, then it is not advisable to go straight onto a raw, whole food diet. This would be too much of a shock to your system. In this case, you should gradually introduce more fresh fruit over a period of six months. This will give your system a chance to know what it's like to work again. In cooking everything we eat, we do the work that the digestive system is supposed to do, and so it gets lazy. If we go back to eating raw foods too quickly, then there will be a period of discomfort and even sickness because we are not able to digest this food easily. And again, with the fasting, take it easy. Try it out for just 24 hours, once per week, and see how you go. Don't jump in (as I usually do) at the deep end.

It's a good idea to gradually phase out breakfast as well. Contrary to common belief, this is *not* the most important meal of the day. In fact, *no meal* is that important; we place far too much emphasis upon eating. When you sleep, your body is eliminating waste. If, after you rise, you keep that elimination process going by not eating and by moving around, which increases the elimination, then you will be taking a short fast every day. Most Westerners are able to give up one meal per day without any problems. We eat too much.

As your body becomes cleaner and is able to function more easily and smoothly, you will find that your brain also functions better. You will be calmer and more easygoing, have no bad thoughts, etc. Such a simple thing as the kind of foods you eat can do so much for you, helping you to become a *real* warrior.

Fruit as Medicine

The ancient Chinese would never eat food just for the sake of eating or satisfying hunger. They treated the food they ate as medicine. The cook, (usually the mother and wife) was not only a cook but also a Chinese doctor. She knew what each member of the family needed to take in to stay healthy. When someone in the family became ill, she would know which foods did what and would prepare something to heal the illness.

I will include only some of the Chinese methods of

treating illness using some of the more common fruits, as it would take a whole book to cover it all.

Some of the following information is based on my own learning, but most of it comes from an excellent book called *Fruit as Medicine*, by Dai Yin-fang and Liu Cheng-jun (translated by Ron Edwards, Rams Skull Press, P/O Box 274, Kuranda, Qld 4872, Australia), and is reprinted here with their kind permission.

The Pear

Many common cough syrups are derivatives of the pear. The ancient Chinese did not have such things as scientists or labs to invent cough syrups; they just used the fruit. You simply take a pear, scoop out some of it and place some honey into that hole. Then bake it! Eat it, and it will help with that persistent cough. It doesn't taste too bad, either.

The pear can also alleviate the effects of too much alcohol and help to cool fevers.

To make a pear medicine, take a pound of pear flesh (no skin or center) and add half a pound of lily bulb (*bulbus lilie*) and some honey. Simmer in water until the mixture thickens.

If you have a burning feeling in the lungs and are perhaps coughing blood with thick phlegm, take one soup - spoon full of pear medicine, morning and evening, every day until the condition has cleared. For a hangover, simply drink two glasses of pear juice.

A warning: do not eat the above if you have a cold feeling in the lungs with a cough, or if you are having trouble with your spleen (the first symptom of this is lack of energy and overall lethargia, but digestive disturbances, abnormal worry, abdominal bloating, muscle prolapse, organ prolapse, varicose veins, and weakness of the immune system in general are all indications of spleen trouble).

The Apple

For indigestion, peel some fresh, half-ripened apple, wrap it in clean gauze, and squeeze to obtain the juice.

Drink half a cupful every four hours, three times during the day.

For hypoglycemia (low blood sugar), peel two fresh apples and eat three times a day for three days.

For vomiting during pregnancy and loss of appetite, stir-fry 40 grams of fresh apple skin and 30 grams of rice till golden, then add water and simmer till cooked. Drink this in place of tea.

For chronic enteritis and/or diarrhea, pour boiling water over 15 grams of dried, powdered apple and serve. Do this twice per day. To make dried, powdered apple, take unripe fruit, cut into quarters, and dry in the sun. When fully dry, crush into powder.

The Orange

For acute throat inflammation, persistent cough, hoarseness, or loss of voice, slowly sip half a cup of fresh orange juice three times a day.

For acute or chronic bronchitis, take one fresh orange, including the skin, cut into four segments, and add 15 grams of honey. Add water and steam for half an hour, then eat, including the skin. Do this in the morning and evening.

For acne, take the seeds of an unripened orange and add a little water, then grind into a paste. Spread on the affected area every evening before going to bed. (Be sure to take it off before going to work or school the next day! No one wants to be called "orange face.")

The Banana

For painful hemorrhoids or bleeding during motion, take two ripened bananas, including the skin, add a little water, steam in a sealed container, and mash. Every day, prepare and eat in the morning and again in the evening, so that you take four bananas a day.

For high blood pressure, take 60 grams of banana skins or stems, steam in water, and eat. Do this three times a day. This can be taken as a preventative as well as a remedy.

For constipation caused by hypertension, mix 500

grams of banana (without the skin) with 15 grams of black sesame seed and eat once a day.

For a hangover, boil 60 grams of banana skin in water and serve.

A warning about bananas: people suffering from stomach ulcers or hyperacidity should avoid eating them, as they are difficult to digest.

Lemon

For tinea (fungus diseases of the skin, particularly ringworm), take one fresh lemon, including the skin, pulp it, wrap it in cotton gauze, and squeeze it to obtain the juice. Apply to the affected area three to four times a day.

For blurred vision or difficulty in adapting vision to the dark, grind 15 grams of lemon seeds to a powder and add boiling water. Every evening take 3 grams, and repeat this for five days.

If you are tired, listless, run-down, and weak, take 3 grams of lemon seeds and crush them to powder. Add 30 grams of rice wine, or *sake*, and take every evening before bed.

Those who suffer from hyperacidity or ulcers should not eat lemons, either.

Figs

The fig is probably one of the best fruits for humans to eat. It cures and helps to cure many disease states. It is particularly good for the colon and all diseases of the colon. I always take some fresh figs with me on the plane when doing a grueling trip overseas (30 hours straight of flying sometimes).

For constipation associated with old age, eat one or two figs every evening before going to bed. (I must add here that constipation should *not* come with old age if we have done all the right things in getting there. Just because we are old does not mean that we should automatically be ill.)

For rheumatism, pains in the joints, etc., take 60 grams of fresh figs, one egg, and 15 grams of rice wine or *sake*. Simmer with water until cooked, and eat once a day. (If this does not work, drink the whole bottle of *sake* and you won't feel anything!)

For warts or tinea, crush several unripe fresh figs and squeeze to obtain the juice. Rub this on the affected area each day.

These are just a few of the more than 150 different fruits and their associated healing capabilities that are listed in *Fruit as Medicine*.

STRUCTURAL THERAPY

Structural therapy, unlike "posture therapy," takes into account the well-being of the whole body, including internal organs, joints, sinews, muscles, etc. The state of the skeleton is a mirror of one's internal health, and anything that is amiss internally shows up structurally somewhere. The way we breathe, the way we walk, the way we talk, the way we hold our limbs, and the way we move all point to what is happening inside.

In order to understand what is happening inside of our bodies, all we need do is to look at the external. It is important, therefore, that we also to know how to interpret, and then diagnose from that interpretation, the state of the structure of the body. For instance, if the lower back is continually "going out," this could indicate something wrong with the colon and elimination organs. It could also indicate some structural damage which, in turn, is affecting the colon. So we get a sort of vicious circle, where an internal problem is affecting the structure, which, in turn, affects the internal organ associated with it.

Stress

One of the major causes of modern structural problems is twentieth-century stress. Stress affects the whole skeletal system, as well as the muscles and internal organs. It will cause the muscles to actually pull bones out of place and hamper the stomach's ability to digest food. Stress is so powerful that it can even cause us to sustain torn ligaments when only the lightest pressure is applied. Muscles and ligaments are extremely resilient and strong, and it takes a great deal of pressure to damage them under normal circumstances. However, if one leads a stressful life and allows that stress to have an adverse effect, the muscles and ligaments will become weakened and buckle under to something that they normally would be able to withstand.

Repetitive Strain Injury (RSI), a stress-related disorder that is becoming increasingly common in Australia, falls into this category. In a normal, happy atmosphere, those tasks which now affect thousands of people adversely each year would have no effect because the stress would not be allowed to enter the muscles and tendons.

Another factor in RSI is the food we eat, which affects the colon. The colon is linked to the forearms, and any disorder in this area also has an effect upon that area, hence RSI. Women seem to be affected by RSI more so than men, and this is because women—especially those in the work force or with executive positions—are much more prone to stress than their male counterparts. This is why we see much more RSI in the female population. In a recent survey conducted to try to understand why many fewer people are affected by RSI in the United States than in Australia, it was found that the work force in the United States is generally a much happier unit than that in Australia. The Americans still eat just as much rubbish affecting the colon, but it appears that this is offset slightly by their happier work atmosphere.

So it can be seen that a person who has RSI could be diagnosed as having something wrong with the colon, which could be remedied by a complete change in diet. This change in diet would also affect the individual's general well-being, resulting in a stronger resistance to stress.

Generally, those who eat less refined sugar and junk food are able to cope much better than those who believe that their stressful condition is caused by a lack of sugar and take more and more. Refined sugar (i.e., the white stuff that TV advertisements tell us is perfectly natural but that does not occur anywhere in nature) causes extreme internal activity, and—as the external is a mirror of the internal—this has to show up somewhere in the structure of the body. It usually shows up first in the shoulders of those who use their hands, such as secretaries or computer operators. Then, as the condition persists, it works its way up the neck to cause headaches and slowly down the arms to cause RSI. Eventually people leave work and rest to try to cure the ailment, blaming it on the kind of work they have to perform, when just a simple change in diet might have cleared up the whole situation.

In order to try to get our structures back to a more normal condition and to offset the ravages of twentieth-century stress, we must start with what we eat. In a nutshell, people who eat less refined sugar and more natural fruit sugars and vegetable matter and, in particular, do not eat to excess, are less prone to stress than those who eat too much food and too much of the wrong kinds of it. In addition to providing some nutritional value as opposed to just "empty calories," fruit sugars and other natural sugars, such as honey, are "slow release," i.e., they have to be burned to be used by the body. Refined sugar, on the other hand, goes straight into the blood and raises the blood sugar very quickly, causing one to experience a short burst of energy, or a "sugar high." The body responds by producing so much insulin that the level of sugar in the blood then plummets. Thus the high is quickly replaced by a "low," and the end result is that we feel tired and lethargic.

The human body is made to receive food that has vitamins, protein, fat, and so on, combined in different ways for a perfect natural balance. When we give the body food that has been altered and robbed of its natural nutritional value (white sugar and white flour being prime examples), we upset this natural balance.

The next area to look at with regard to stress is the way we breathe. Someone who is affected by stress can be diagnosed easily based on the way he or she breathes. Generally, stress affects the way we breathe in two ways:

the quickness of the breath and the stress of the chest in general. If, upon inhalation, there is a great lifting of the chest and a drawing in of the lower abdomen, then stress is likely to be present.

The whole of Western society has caused us to become a race of "upper body" people. Little attention is given to the lower body, bar perhaps what shoes we wear. TV advertisements for cosmetics, hair products, and clothes all point to the upper part of the body. Who ever thinks of what is under their feet! As a consequence, our whole being and awareness are pushed to an upper level, unbalancing the whole structure internally and psychically.

This causes us to breathe incorrectly, using the upper chest only so that we "look good" (thin torso, filled-out chest, etc.), when all the time we are weakening the basic structure by causing a yang-developed upper and a yin-developed lower body. Normally, the lower part, the part that holds us up, should be the yang part, while the upper body should be loose and flexible, or yin. So internally, in terms of energy, we are turning ourselves upside down through wrong thinking. The tendency to breathe with the upper part of our bodies means that we use only a small part of the upper lung area, which causes us to breathe more rapidly, resulting in high blood pressure and heart ailments, which are signs of stress. (I have found through my own practice that women, again, tend to have more breathing troubles than men.)

Changing the way we breathe is not an easy task. Relaxation is such an easy word, but it is so difficult for most people to understand. Relaxation will not only cure your wrong breathing, it will also cure your stress condition. When I talk of relaxation, I do not mean taking a holiday or sitting in your favorite chair in front of the TV. Whole-structure relaxation, internal and external, comes with dedicating many hours to reversing the effects of things that we have done wrong all of our lives. Our muscles have become so tense that when we think we are relaxed, we are really still in a state of extreme tension, with the muscles unable to release.

Many factors can affect the body's ability to relax completely. On a physical level, we can get a massage, take up t'ai chi, or practice qigong. We can also use our minds. The mind is our strongest ally to curing stress.

Once again, if your whole upper body is relaxed, then there is only one way you can breathe, and that is the natural way, allowing the lower abdomen to expand as the lungs fill up and then contract as the air is released, deflating like a balloon. There is simple exercise you can do to gain this ability. Lie on your bed or on the floor and raise your knees so that your whole back is flat, with no hollow underneath the lower back. Place your palms onto your lower abdomen and completely relax your upper chest and shoulders. As you breathe in, say to yourself, "I'm going to make my hands raise up when I breathe in" (fig. 321). With a little practice, you will be able to breathe naturally again, and the effect upon your whole structure will be great.

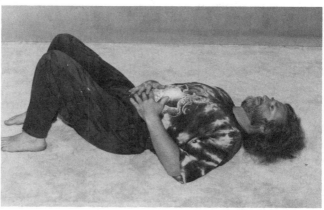

Figure 321

Looseness of the Joints and Ligaments

Many of us go through life wondering what is wrong with us, when some simple exercises to loosen the joints would make a world of difference. The internal organs need to be massaged just as much as the external structure does. Many animals have this ability built in to their structures so that when they move, their internal organs receive a total massage.

Because of the way we have evolved (I use this term lightly), we have forgotten about the ligaments in modern times. If we do not have elastic ligaments, our whole movement is restricted, and thus the internal organs do not receive the attention they need to act accordingly. Flexible ligaments mean flexible joints. If joints did not have ligaments, they would be able move through their full range of motion. There are, of course, limitations upon any joint. If we try to move it somewhere it is not supposed to go, then we actually wear away the bones. The following are some easy exercises to help with ligament flexibility.

The Neck

Not too much work is needed with the neck, as it is obviously quite sensitive. This exercise will also affect the small intestine and improve digestion.

Figure 322

Stand with both feet flat and knees slightly bent, palms placed with fingers linked around the back of your neck. Keeping the body straight ahead and only moving the head, rotate the head as far as it will go without too much strain. Your palms will slip as your neck moves, so that they stay in the same position. *Do not force your head too far. Your chin should be able to go almost to your shoulder, but not right over it* (fig. 322). Breathe in as you turn and hold this posture for about five seconds and then return your head to straight on as you breathe out. Repeat on the other side.

The Arms, Shoulders, Chest, and Back

"Praying backward" lightly stretches the shoulder ligaments. This affects the gall bladder and large intestine, thus improving elimination as well as the breakdown of fats.

Stand as before and touch your palms together around your back area. Move the palms upward until they touch (fig. 323). Open your shoulders to the back as you breathe in, hold this for about five seconds, and then release with the out breath. This will also improve the capacity of the lungs.

The "double snake" posture exercises the ligaments that attach your arms to your body and has an effect upon the heart and lungs. It also increases

Figure 323

Figure 324

Figure 325

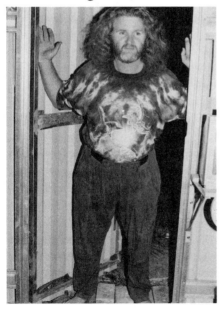

Figure 326

the general flexibility of the whole chest and back area. Stand as before and wrap your right arm under your left elbow. Now snake your right palm up so that you are able to link your hands (fig. 234). If you are unable to do this, hold onto a tea towel or the like, and slowly pull your palms together (fig. 325).

To open the whole chest area and exercise the rib ligaments, stand in a doorway and place your palms onto the sides. Push your body forward and feel the pressure on your upper arms. Breathe in and hold for a few seconds; relax it as you breathe out (fig. 326).

For flexibility of the wrist ligaments, which acts upon the colon, use your palms to walk down a wall, keeping your back and your legs straight and your palms flat against the wall (fig. 327). Repeat this with the backs of your palms.

Take note of any

267

severe pain and desist in any of these exercises. It could indicate an internal problem or just severe inflexibility in the joints, and overdoing the exercises could damage the ligaments.

The Waist and Hips

There is a difference between the waist and the hips. Waist movement is everything above the sacrum bone, while hip movement is everything below it.

This first exercise works upon the whole backbone, thus toning up the central nervous system and exercising just about every other organ.

Stand with a stick over your shoulders with palms laying across the stick. Turn your upper body to the left and to the right as far as you can go without pain. *Turn only as far as your waist will allow you to!* A little tight feeling is okay. Do not allow your hips to move; keep them straight ahead. Start this momentum and

Figure 327

Figure 328

Figure 329

allow the natural movement of the stick to take you. Do not allow your legs to move (fig. 328).

By increasing the flexibility of the hips, this exercise affects your rejuvenation factors—thus keeping you looking young and healthy—as well as the elimination organs.

Stand with feet parallel and about shoulder width apart. You can use the stick over your shoulders while standing in a doorway to stop your upper body from moving. Try to rotate your hips as far as they will go, which won't be very far, as the hips are not that flexible naturally (fig. 329). This exercise also tends to bring your whole body back into alignment.

The Legs and Pelvis

For the ball joints between your legs and pelvis, stand on one leg and rotate the other leg, first in a clockwise direction and then in a counterclockwise direction. Do this until you feel the strain on your standing leg at the ball joint. This will affect your general well-being, as well as keep you young. It acts upon the sexual organs (fig. 330).

With all of the above exercises, you should breathe deeply, but do not force it. Keep your whole body relaxed and do not allow more tension to creep in, thus negating what you are trying to achieve with this set. Spending just a little time each morning on these exercises will enhance your overall well-being by simply starting to fight stress.

Take a look at yourself; in particular, your upper body.

Look with your peripheral vision and try to take in the whole body without focusing. See if your shoulders are nicely rounded and hanging, as in Figure 331, or if they are held up by tension. If the latter is the case, you should try to remedy the situation by simply thinking about it. Be aware of when your shoulders are tense. This usually comes about when you are placed in a stressful situation. It could be simply driving the car, or watching something violent on television. You must realize what your limitations to stress are, and then you will become aware of your own stress and so defeat it.

Figure 330

In order to call oneself a warrior, one must first of all be healthy in body, mind, and spirit. All of the above will help you on your way toward that goal of becoming a true warrior.

Figure 331

The Way of the Warrior

11

A warrior is not just a person who has learned some moves, is able to kick at 90 mph, or has won the world kickboxing championships. A warrior must earn his title. The martial artist is a person who knows things that go far deeper than just self-defense. He is someone who walks into a room full of people and an immediate calm falls upon that room. He is a person who can touch a person's head, arm, or hand and cause an inner stillness and peace to fall upon that person. You know a warrior not from the way he looks, his big biceps, his rolled-up sleeves revealing a row of tattoos, his shaven head, or the fact that he wears his full gi (karate uniform) to parties!

We know the warrior by his presence and the healing he automatically gives to everyone he meets. His energy, his qi, is touching you. You don't feel anything physical, but rather the internal effect of this touching, and peace is with you.

The warrior looks upon the Earth in a different way than those who are not warriors. Everything, from the smallest insect to the largest mammal to the most insignificant rock or tree, is important and has life: the grass he thanks for softening the rough path he walks upon; the trees he thanks for giving him shade and oxygen. Everything has importance because it was put there by Mother Earth for some reason.

Sure, he has to live in modern times; he must drive a motorcar and go to the supermarket and mow his lawns, but he never loses sight of what he is and, more importantly, where he is. He knows he is not only what he has made himself to be, but also all that his ancestors have handed down to him, which has accumulated right inside the very cells he is made of. Everything that they were is now him. Every bit of information that his father and mother gathered is now inside of him.

This is how we live on in our children. We literally—and I mean literally—pass on our knowledge, along with tons of knowledge accumulated since the beginning of time, to our children. Everything that we are at the time of our children's conception is passed on to them. We think that we have certain talents, but the warrior knows that all that he is has come from the beginning of time.

He knows that he is made up of the same stuff that a rock is made of, or a tree, or a blade of grass; the difference is only physical. He knows that he owns nothing and that all animals are free. His animals choose him to be with. He does not go to the pet shop to choose a new dog; he knows that the dog has chosen him to come to that pet shop to choose it.

The warrior communicates with the Earth; he talks to the dogs, to the cats and owls, to the snakes—not so much verbally, but simply by being. This is the one thing that everything on Earth has in common: being. He knows that there are forces at work on this Earth, forces that he must learn to go with and to live with, otherwise he will surely perish. The energy within the warrior gives him the power to join these forces, and then he has the power to change. But this comes not without payment, for he also knows that we cannot receive something without first having paid for it. The whole of the universe is based upon this giving and taking; it is called yin and yang. For every up there must be a down, for every happiness, there must be a sadness, for every full tummy, there must be an empty one.

The warrior knows that he must lose in order to gain, and so he sacrifices. He sacrifices his food, his sexual longings, his everyday comforts, so that he has the power to change and to help others change. It's not that he goes out specifically to help others, but he always has the internal power there to automatically help others to be peaceful and, in doing so, help them, too, to be able to see where they are and who they are.

We are not only someone's son or daughter. We are the sons and daughters of an infinite number of people, all of who have passed on to us the material within their cells, inside of which is hidden the very substance of creation and everything that has happened for infinity.

Being a martial artist is only a fraction of what a warrior is. It is only a part of the whole. It is what gives us the confidence to become healers, the internal energy to make changes.

The warrior learns to communicate other than by speaking. He knows that we do not have teachers, but guides—the people we meet who are able to give us something internal, that something extra to cause us to become our own greatest teachers. Just by simply being, a guide helps us to realize that it is we who teach ourselves. The warrior also knows that locked away inside of everything is that primordial cell that contains all information. He learns to read this information, which comes in the form of "flashes" at first, and because this is too much for his feeble human brain to handle, he shuts off as soon as the flash arrives. But soon he learns to read these flashes, and they become longer in duration than just a moment. This is when the warrior knows that he is reading time.

A warrior knows that his physical needs are being looked after and needs not worry about where the next mortgage payment will come from. The warrior finds his place on the Earth and stays there, where the power is. It is not a physical searching, but rather the warrior is "taken" to where he must be, and there he stays, and the whole world will pass by. He needs not to travel, because the universe is there within him, and those who will in turn need to seek him out will do so when their time is right, in the same way that he did when he had to travel the world searching for his own guides. They will learn then to teach themselves from within, and go and find their own place, and he may never see them again. But this does not worry the warrior; he is in contact.

The warrior is not the master, he is not the sifu nor the sensei. These are just physical words that we put upon ourselves to make us seem important or better than those whom we guide. The warrior is a friend to his students, and so cannot be their master. He does not wish to gather students, as they will search him out. And those who need to have a master or a sensei will not stay; they will keep searching until they realize that what they seek is within them, and who they seek can only be their guide.

Philosophy

12

There was once this old chap who knew a lot. He had gained this information through experience and living. Someone suggested that it would be a good idea for him to write it all down. He did so, and what came out was nothing like what he intended or what he was really thinking about internally. This is what happened with one of the greatest Chinese "philosophers," Lao-tze.

Lao-tze is to Chinese thought and the Taoist religion what Jesus is to Christianity. He was forced to write down what he knew, and hence the whole of Taoist thought comes from those writings. I guess if Jesus Christ and Lao-tze came back in human form today, they would be horrified at what is being taught in their names.

Such is the way of philosophy—write it down and it becomes just that, a bunch of words, and eventually those words can become a religion with millions of adepts around the world.

It is my belief that philosophy cannot be learned from a book. Philosophy comes from inside a person; it is the sum of that person's life experience. When something is written down, it becomes translatable, and everyone who reads that mystical work will have a different interpretation of its meaning, based upon their own lives.

Take the Chinese artist who draws or paints a great work of art, then rolls it up and places it on a shelf for no one to see but himself. Years later, he unrolls that work of art, and he is prompted as to what it was he was thinking about way back then. It is not for others to see, only the painter. The work of art is an expression of his philosophy from within.

So it is with the great philosophers. They write something down, and others read it (maybe thousands of years later) with reference to their own lives and their own time, and not the life and time of the one who wrote it in the beginning.

Philosophy should be shown. It should be passed on from teacher to student, from great mind to pupil—only by someone who is able to transmit the *internal essence* of what he has learned in life. Everyone who has "lived" has formed some ideas about life over the years, and those ideas make up that person's philosophy; no one else's. That person is able to "show" these ideas through the way he or she lives—not by preaching to others, but by doing. He acts as an example of what he believes in, and others may or may not follow this example. The sage does not care whether or not anyone follows his teachings or ideas. To care would be to have ego. The sage does what he has to, what he is "told" to do by his own voices from within. If no one even listens to him, he does not care. He has done his job and has therefore fulfilled his reason for being.

CHILDREN

One's ideas (and not one's philosophy or experience from within) *can* be written down, as these are physical things that the student can follow in order to gain his or her own philosophy. In knowing our own philosophy, we then know our reason for being. And when we know our reason for being, nothing else matters; we are doing what God meant us to do.

I guess if I have any philosophy of my own, it would be called "the philosophy of children and family." We, as adults, sometimes lose sight of the real values of life, due to our ideas of our own importance. But we only exist to teach our children! (Children are classified in the martial arts as our students as well as our own children.) What other reason do we have for existence? Is it to invent a better television? Or a new kind of car? Apart from keeping ourselves alive by going to work each day, our reason for being lies in our children, without whom there would *be* no future. We all know that the children are the future of our world, but how may of us *really* believe this? We say it, but do we really think it? Whenever someone perhaps writes something silly about me in an article (and I have been slandered by the best of them), I do not allow it to affect me, but rather I look at my children, and then I know why I am here.

I have a favorite saying: "What's the use of living if we have to die?" (I think I made that up myself.) So there must be some way that we live on. And there is. We live on in our children. We give to them not only physical things, but also internal ideas and chemical things that have literally been passed to them via our cells. If we could look into a cell and translate what was written there, we would be able to see back infinitely and forward infinitely. I have noticed it with my own five children. Everything that myself and my wife (and my first wife) were when they were conceived was passed on to them, and as I am constantly changing, all of my children are completely different.

We subconsciously pass on, through our cells, our philosophy. No need to write it down; it is passed on to those who need it automatically. That learning process continues all the child's life, even after we die. Our influence as parents continues to nurture and protect our children.

And then that influence is again passed on in their cells to their children. So what we are, and what our children are, is the sum of all of our ancestors' philosophies right back to the beginning of human life.

INFINITY

Sometimes we have "flashes." These are instant and minute learning periods that we get as we come to know what our own philosophies actually are. The things we learn in these flashes cannot be written down, or even thought about afterward; they are meant for our subconscious minds. But as the subconscious and our conscious minds come closer together as a result of life's experiences, etc., the conscious mind catches a glimpse of these flashes. Many times it is just too much for the conscious, trapped human mind to take, and we must shut it off immediately. It's as if a door opens for a split second, something wonderful comes in, and then the door is closed again. Like when we're waiting for someone at the airport, the automatic doors open and we are able, for a brief time, to look inside at all the people coming through customs, etc. We gaze at the wondrous and secretive things that lie on the other side of the door, and then it closes. This is the way of a flash.

Infinity is one of the things that we learn about in these sessions. Our feeble human brains just cannot comprehend infinity. It means nothing. It means the Tao. For something to just keep on going and going with no beginning and no ending is just incredible. One of my older sons just could not understand this concept. He kept saying that there must have been a beginning. I kept answering him that in order for something to have a beginning, there must have been something before it. And in order for something to have an ending, there must be something after it. Beginnings and endings cannot exist without something before or after; otherwise, we could not have a beginning and an ending.

During some flashes, we get a glimpse of infinity, and I'm telling you that it is, well, nothing! Too big—no, not big, because it cannot have size. Size can only ever be relevant to something else. Here I am, trying to write down something that is not even speakable. When one has this brief encounter with infinity, nothing else matters. Governments, mortgages, disasters, and so forth are all irrelevant. The only thing that does matter, always, is love.

LEARNING

The way we learn the martial arts is the way we learn anything. It should be a natural experience. The following is what I believe to be the right way to learn, based upon my own experience, and that is a physical way of "doing" in order to come upon one's own philosophy from within.

My children from my current and final marriage do not go to school; they never have. They are not even "schooled" at home. They learn at home, and some people call this "home schooling." I prefer to simply call it learning. One of the most unnatural things on earth is to sit down and do math problems. Why? There is no reason for doing this. We force our little children to do unnatural acts.

Learning should be nothing special; it should be no different than our normal daily activities. In this way, what we learn becomes an "experience" and is taken into the mind properly, rather than in parrot fashion. For instance, rather than sit my children down at a table with a book of arithmetic, I take them with me when I do my financial things. From the time he was 7 years old, Ben, my eldest (living with me, that is; I have two others who are, at the time of this writing, 24 and 23 years old) would do the banking for me. He would, and still does do, the international money conversions and write the daily checks into the deposit book. I do not have to do anything! Little Eli, 6 years old, is also doing the banking and postage for me each day. I take them to do the daily shopping in town, and they must do the various sums to work out change, etc. This is *living* math, and totally natural. It's the same with anything they learn—it is done for a reason. But more importantly, it is nothing different from what they do each day. We do not have a special time when we do math or spelling or writing or science. If it's there, we learn it. There might be a small marsupial hole when we go on one of our walks through our rain forest. We examine this, measure it, find out what has been eaten, etc. This is also living learning. The children will remember this experience. If I were to sit them down and give them a natural science lesson, they would have to do that particular lesson over and over again in order for the information to go in.

All of the children assist in the making of a new garden. Little Kataleena, who is only 2, helps in everything, no matter how difficult the task. She likes to place the new plants into their holes, etc. At times we have three children playing away on the piano. Sandra and I have to stop them from doing too much. They're probably the only kids in the world who come to *us* and demand that we give them music lessons! This is the way it should be with the martial arts. There is no special time for doing it.

Someone once asked me what he should do to prepare to do his taiji. I told him that there is no preparation. He should be ready to do it at any time; his body should just tell him when it is ready to perform the kata. You might be brushing your teeth. You put your toothbrush down, do your kata, and resume cleaning your teeth, as if nothing different has happened. Only in this way does your martial art become a part of your life, a part of *you*.

Many people like to "dress up" when they do their martial arts, because it makes them feel more like they are "doing" a martial art. Some even go so far as to dress up in old Chinese garb that was in vogue long before their particular martial art was even invented! Real Chinese masters look at some of us in the West doing our taiji or bagwa or h'sin-i, and they laugh at what we wear. The Chinese only wear uniforms when they do tournaments. This is obviously so that each team can be recognized easily. Apart from that, they do their martial arts in their normal clothes on the way to work, or on the way home, etc. The Chinese of old used to do their martial arts in the normal clothes of the time. Nowadays, we see photos of these people back then, and assume that this is their costume! So, 100 years later, we in the West wear a dress, an old Chinese dress, to do our martial arts! Silly.

My teacher, Chang Yiu-chun, told me that I must *become* taiji; I must not *do it*. We have all heard that we must be doing our martial art all the time. This does not mean that we walk in a certain way, or try to be aware of potential attackers. It means that we must make the martial art so internal that we move flowingly. We are calm at all times. We do not allow things to upset us, no matter what. This is what the martial arts teach us at the highest level. We learn (experience) internal healing. But we do not learn this by doing anything special; we simply *do* the martial arts.

THE PURPOSE OF THE MARTIAL ARTS

The purpose of the martial arts is not so that we can walk around the street or the dojo with signs all over our clothes or (gi) saying "SENSEI" or "SIFU." You've all seen people who do this. It's as if they have to be recognized as being the leader—an ego thing. The true martial artist does not "look" like a martial artist. He or she is just like any other person on the street. He does not show off by wearing certain clothing. Ego should not be a part of one's martial art. To be egotistical, one must be egotistical about something. If our martial art is a normal part of our lives, then it is nothing special, so we cannot be egotistical about it or ourselves.

The highest level of the martial arts is to heal. The fighting is only the initial work that men, in particular, need to do to overcome their insecurities. (Men seem to have a thousand more insecurities than women.) We have to get over that huge hurdle of showing others that we are king of the roost, that we can defend ourselves. I guess this goes back to when we used to live in caves and had to literally fight for our lives daily, or fight for the women, etc. We do not have to do this nowadays, but the internal thought is still there. Look at any animal families (we have plenty of those on our farm). The male of the species is constantly fighting other males of the same species. And it's usually over the females or the food. We, as human beings do not need to do this! But we must get over that feeling of insecurity, hence our learning the martial arts. This is not a bad thing, though. It gives we males more confidence in life and in business, and it gives females a little more confidence in simply walking down the street. (That is the way of the times, unfortunately. Just take a look at the TV video programs available in most expensive hotels around the world, and I have stayed in more than a few. What do you see more listings of? X-rated movies. This is the sad road that we men, mainly, have come down. And this is why women have to learn the martial arts.)

A person in the United States was interviewed by one of his students for an article that was published in one of the British martial arts magazines. I had previously stated in an article that what this particular person was doing in demonstration was dangerous (in a nutshell, striking anywhere in the neck area, especially the carotid sinus), and I introduced some of the world's leading healing people to substantiate my claims. This person said that I was wrong to bring healers into the argument, because they had nothing to do with the martial arts; martial arts and healing were completely different!

A martial artist cannot be a martial artist and not know about healing. In days gone by, this was the first area that a martial artist learned, and was considered to be the highest level of the martial arts. It seems that many modern so-called masters have only taken a small part of the original (from China) martial arts training and left the rest. Then they grade themselves up to a master or grand master degree. Even in the original Okinawan karate, the students were taught the healing side of their often deadly strikes.

The healing side of the martial arts is not only the most important, but also the most difficult to learn. It's easy to learn to strike someone in the neck to knock them out, but much more difficult to learn how to heal using those same points. It takes much more brainpower and a certain amount of intelligence to learn this part.

Most Chinese masters used either acupuncture or dim-mak as their healing art. The shorinji kempo karate people used shiatsu, a finger-pressure healing art derived from the dim-mak points that were used in the martial area. Many today use Chinese herbs, bone manipulation, or energy-flow therapeutics to heal. I tend to use the dim-mak points with finger pressure, Chinese bone setting, and energy-flow therapy, along with the occasional Tui-na, or Chinese massage.

But it's not just the physical healing that a martial artist does. His or her whole being is healing. Just being there has an effect on people. His own energy is able to calm and heal, simply by being close. A touch of a hand is able to cause healing, with no special movements on the part of the healer. Just a shaking of the hand is sometimes sufficient to cause a healing in someone. This is the true nature and reason for being of the martial arts.

To Know a Real Martial Artist

Just look at him. Very overweight? Gi too tight? Skin not healthy looking, eyes not sparkling? This is not a martial artist.

A calm nature is the first thing to look for—someone who communicates with you rather than just talking with you or at you as many do in seminars. Martial artists communicate on different levels of energy. They have magnetic personalities, simply because of the internal training. This means that their level of qi is normal, and more of it emits from the body, communicating with the qi of others. Look at his health first, *then* look to see if he can fight. Of course, a martial artist must know how to defend himself and also be able to show others how to do likewise. If, for instance, you never actually see him doing any self-defense, but rather just asking people to stand in front of him and then performing techniques on them, then this is not a martial artist. If the martial artist asks people from the seminar or workshop to actually attack him, using any method of attack, and *then* shows how he defends himself, then this is usually a good indicator that the person knows his stuff. It has nothing to do with how many tournaments he has been in; this is not real fighting.

CHANG YIU-CHUN ON PHILOSOPHY: THE CLASSICS AND THE TAO TE CHING

The *Tao Te Ching* is a book supposedly written by a person called Lao-Tze (Lau Tzzoo). This book and its author can be likened to the Bible and Jesus. It is said that this great philosopher was leaving on his ox to die in the hills, when he was forced by a border guard to write down his philosophy of life. And the *Tao Te Ching* is what came from this encounter. He did not wish to write it all down, because he knew that his philosophy was his own, and no one else's. And, as with the Bible, who knows who has added to it over the years.

My own ideas on the classics come from those of Chang Yiu-chun. His ideas on just about everything were just about as radical as one could get where taiji was concerned. This I liked, because it was so totally different from anything I had ever learned or read in the past. His ideas on the "classics" are just as radical.

The classics are a bunch of sayings and advice given by some of the most revered taiji masters of the past. In most cases, they are all we have to go upon, so how we interpret them is of great importance. Some have interpreted them literally, while others have taken a more "internal" approach to their execution. Chang goes even further. The following includes some excerpts of conversations I had with Chang wherein he shared some of his ideas on the classics and other things.

Chang: Yes, I have read those things [classics] once or twice. My teacher [Yang Shou-hou] never even told me about them. It was long after he died that I was given a book with some words written in about taijiquan, that I knew about these classics. No, I never took much notice of them. If one has learned correctly, then one does not need such classics. I also read the words of Lao-tze. I think that he must have been a funny man. I would like to have known him. Many people have made a whole religion up based on his words, and I hear many people making [saying] his words to others to show how much they know about Taoist philosophy. They say that we must do what Lao-tze says that we must do in his book the *Tao Te Ching* and what a good person he must have been.

Lao-tze was neither a good or a bad person. He knew not of such things. He was just a person who had much internal experience. Those who take his words literally are missing the greatest gift to us from Lao-tze, and that is that we should not take what he has written down literally. I believe that Lao-tze was forced to write down what he knew before he disappeared. Such an advanced brain immediately knew what to do in such a situation. He left us some physical words. He knew that those who came after would be able to work out the riddle of his words. All he was trying to tell us in all of his writings was, "Look what I have found in my brain! You too are able to find such wondrous things."

EM: Lao-tze just wanted to tell us that we should look inward to ourselves and find what is written in our own minds.

He did not want us to follow his every word and to make a religion upon them. He just wanted to tell us that we should look inward to ourselves and find what is written in our own minds. Probably, we will find exactly the same things that he discovered in there, but it is for every person to find his own way, and not go the way of someone else. Everyone has his own religion, which cannot be given or taught to anyone else.

On another occasion, I asked Chang about health matters.

Chang: Health is a word. People make a lot of money from that word. Health should be just people. This is what we are—health! If the humans had not gone on the track that we have gone on, we would not need such words as health. In the beginning, when people came, there was food. Plenty of food for everyone. That food was the stuff that also kept the human machine in good order. We knew no other way, and our deaths would come not from ill health, but from wild animals attacking and eating us. The stuff that we were eating was the stuff that was there. Now, we go to the supermarket and eat things that are months old. We eat things that were not there in the beginning, things that humans have made for us to eat, and not what was given to us to eat.

In a way, I am happy that people have gone along the road that they have, because now we have things like taijiquan to help us to get well. We need taijiquan because of the strange things that we do to ourselves. Just think how "well" we would be if we also put into ourselves what was there in the beginning, just food, and also practiced our taijiquan!

I had an occasion to meet a person in China who could not move. She was having to have everything done for her and was told that she would not live for long. I taught this person taijiquan in her mind for some years and made her a diet of food. After many years she could still not move. But she was alive. I think that she also had a new bed.

Just about everything that I do nowadays has that same radical feel to it that Chang had. And I think that was what he was really trying to show me—not so much the physical, but what was inside of me already.

And, please, in years to come, long after I am gone, do not pick up this book and invent a religion based upon what I have written in this chapter. Work it out for yourself; it's all in there.

Dim-Mak for Children

13

"If you wish to give your children the best start in life, don't give them money, don't give them schooling, don't give them a job, don't give them a house and a car. Just give them real love; the rest will then naturally follow."

—Erle Montaigue

Even a child can do something about defending himself against an attacker. My own son Ben was able to knock me out at 8 years of age. (We did this regularly to find out what points worked easily and which ones did not work so easily.) Ben is now 10 years old and wanting to learn more and more, and he will become my true successor (as it was in ancient China, with the son of the son of the son carrying on the family martial art). Eli, age 7, is also coming along nicely, as is Kataleena, age 2, who's just hitting everyone with swords and sticks right now and will begin her training at age 4.

The small person is able to use dim-mak to make up for any shortcomings in strength and size. Often, the smaller person (child) will have a distinct advantage, in that an attacker does not expect retaliation. So the attacker is off guard from the start. A child must be taught not to struggle in the beginning when attacked, abducted, etc. The child must wait for his or her chance, when the attacker is completely confident that this little person is incapable of attack. Then, he or she must attack with such ferocity to death points that the attacker will be killed or maimed—or at the very least incapacitated for long enough

Figure 332

to give the child time to escape. This is possible. I have felt the attacks of children who aren't afraid, and given the correct points, they can be lethal.

Often people will accuse me of training my children to kill. I say, "Yes, I am!" In these unfortunate times, it is necessary for every child to be able to do something. The world is becoming like it was back in ancient China, when one *had* to be able to fight for one's life. The whole family would be trained in survival arts.

In Australia, in the state of New South Wales at least (some states do not allow home schooling), we can get legal permission to teach our children at home. The inspector (of schools) comes around and has a friendly chat with the family, just to see if the parents aren't complete idiots, and then gives an exemption from school. On our first meeting with the inspector, after giving all the right reasons for wishing to home-school, I asked Ben to do his stuff (kicks, punches, locks and holds, etc.). I asked the inspector if he would send a kid like that to school. He just shook his head and said, "exemption granted."

Many make the big mistake of trying to teach children too formally, like being in school. As I stated in the chapter on philosophy, learning must be a natural process, a natural part of daily life. This is even more important when teaching children the martial arts. Force them to bow at the door and call you sensei, discipline them for talking in the dojo, etc., and you will lose them completely.

It's like the child who is forced to take piano lessons. It becomes a chore, and any interest the child once had in playing the piano is squelched. However, if that child's whole family is taking piano lessons as a part of everyday life, with the piano being used most of the day by the whole family on and off, then the learning becomes just like playing—nothing special; it's a part of life. So, too, must the martial arts become a part of life.

So many parents send their children to a karate class in order to get rid of them for a couple of hours. This is like sending them to school! The whole family must get involved in the learning so that the child sees that this is something natural and not different. In our case, the children see the martial arts all the time. Everyone who comes to our house is in some way involved in the martial arts. The children see my wife Sandra and me practicing; they see our students/friends come for training. The talk usually comes around to the martial arts, and they hear this as being normal.

Sadly, though, there are few teachers who know how to teach children. The classes are usually either too free, where the children simply run amuck, or they are too stiff and disciplined. Both approaches are wrong for children. They are wrong for adults, too. How many times have you heard, "They need the discipline." Who needs it? We have too much discipline as it is. So how does one get children to behave, so that everyone in the class is able to learn? By being firm but friendly and by treating the child exactly the same way that the adults are treated.

By respecting the child. In this way, the child will respect you as the teacher.

WHAT CAN A CHILD DO?

There is no difference between what I teach to adults and what I teach to children. All that children need be taught is that they *can* do it. Once they know that it is not beyond their often small frames, then the learning is easy.

I teach children straight up—the most deadly points. I speak to them as adults and tell them that this is not a game; it could mean that they will be able to save their lives or those of their sisters or brothers. And above all, the art must never be used to show off. Most children warm to this type of teaching and are responsible enough to understand that they are capable of killing an adult. I notice an immediate change in children once they truly know that they have the ability in their hands to kill. They become quieter and more responsible. But then, this is what the martial arts are all about—giving more confidence and character. The confidence and character do not come from knowing how to kick or punch, but rather from knowing what these techniques can do.

I teach the points first. Each member of my family, including the children, is adept at massage. Through this, the children have learned about points. They think it's fun to make Daddy jump! My wife's sister Jenny is an expert in Chinese massage and Chinese healing in general. When she comes to visit, the children run to her to find out the next massage technique. So right from the beginning they are learning an integrated system of martial art, which includes the healing areas.

When Ben was smaller, I taught him the claw. His little fingers became so strong at clawing away at soft tissue that I had difficulty in holding him. He would dig his fingers into the soft tissue on either side of the abdomen, which is a wonderful technique to cause someone to let go. It is especially effective when they do not expect it. At

Figure 333

Figure 334

present I have a scar over my right eye from little Kataleena, who at 2 years of age knows that if she claws her little fingernails into Daddy's eyes, he will jump and yell! Our house is like an integrated training area with not one but three "Katos" (from the *Pink Panther* movies).

The carotid sinus is the first area of the body that I teach to children. I show it to them, get them to feel it and press it gently. Then I train their hands to strike by allowing them to strike me in protected areas. This is essential to give the child an idea of what it is like to strike a human being (and a large one at that). All the bag training in the world is no substitute for the real thing. Actually, the male joey (baby kangaroo) does exactly this with his mother. She sits there patiently while he hammers away at her with his rear legs. This is important for him to

293

learn how to fight for when he fights for leadership of the pack.

When the child is striking heavily enough, I then take him or her on to learn about techniques. This area kids love, as they think that finally they are learning something real. I give them a training method to learn about the carotid sinus—the same one I gave for this purpose in the chapter for law enforcement officers. In Figure 333, I strike at Ben's head with a hook punch, and he slams my arm and strikes to the carotid sinus. I attack the children in various ways to show them how they should react in such situations. For instance, if they are grabbed and lifted up, they should always wait their moment. Then they should decide on the weapon they should use and, at the right time, slam their fist or palm into the carotid sinus (fig. 334). I then teach chil-

Figure 335

Figure 336

Figure 337

dren about the other lethal points, the ones that work more easily, like Cv 22 (pit of the neck), as shown in Figure 335, or Gv 26 (under the nose), as shown in Figure 336. And if they still do not believe that they can do it, I allow them to practice on me under controlled conditions, with a nurse (my wife) there on hand should anything go wrong. Ben is particularly good at striking to Triple Warmer 23. This was the first point that he struck for real to knock me out, and even I was surprised at how little pressure he had to use. It also has to do with the smallness of children's palms. They seem to bite into the points more easily (fig. 337).

Often two brothers or a brother and sister will come to the class as children. This is the best possible way for children to learn, when they have someone with whom to practice all the time at home. It's important here to stress that when one is older and bigger than the other, he or she should compensate. And at all times, it should be made clear that they are not training to compete with each other; they must only train if they are willing to help each other. Ben and Eli train fighting for many hours each day. This could be with sticks or barehanded, and when one gets struck, usually accidentally (and sometimes on purpose!), they have to help each other with the injury. A terrific bond builds up between children in a family who learn in this way. (Figure 338 shows Ben and Eli training in small san-sau, and Figure 339 shows them training in stick fighting.) And all of this training has come about because they want to do it. If they do not wish to train, then they are not forced to. Same with their piano—if they do not wish to practice, they are not forced to. But invariably, it is they who force *us* to teach them! Figure 340 shows that one is never too young to learn self-defense.

Figure 338

I am often scolded by my wife for teaching the children too much and for allowing them to actually strike me, sometimes to the point where I am mildly hurt. But the children *must* know what it is like to actually strike a person. That way they know exactly how much

Figure 339

Figure 340

power to use and where to hit. If they are only ever striking softly in the training hall, then they never really know that feeling of striking someone for real. Figure 341 shows Kataleena striking me with the stick. This sort of training is the most important that children can do, because it gives them the confidence to know that they can do it.

Figure 341

Some Words of Wisdom from the Master

Chang Yiu-chun was my main teacher in the internal arts. I met him down by the docks in Sydney when I was a chauffeur. I would see this old man practicing something that looked like taiji, and eventually I plucked up enough courage to get out of the limo and watch. He would not acknowledge that I was there; not even when I did my own taiji form in my chauffeur's outfit would he look. After many months, I was able to gain his attention by performing some faster forms. This aroused the ego that was still left in him.

I then discovered that he was one of only three students of Yang Shou-hou, the grandson of the founder of Yang-style taiji who had never changed the style that Yang Lu-Ch'an invented way back then. I had already been investigating this style and was not too far off at that stage.

Chang gave me much more than just the physical movements; he let me watch him doing "nothing." The following comes from my now-fading but readable notes, taken from my brief but greatly informative time with Chang.

Not having the knowledge that we now have from modern science, the old Chinese masters could only say what they felt or were told about. This is how the "classics" of taiji were written—with a lot of feeling, but not much scientific evidence. Nowadays, we have access to a plethora of scientific information, and when we think back to what that old master told us years ago, we can correlate what he said with what is being discovered by scientists now.

It's the same with what Chang Yiu-chun told me. Sometimes he would speak in what I thought then to be riddles, but what now translate as hard scientific fact. So we can take what the old Chinese masters were talking about and juxtapose that knowledge with modern science to come up with reasons for being.

I am now able to relate everything that Chang said to me when I trained with him both to the classics and to modern science.

> **EM:** Tell me about the self-defense of taiji.
> **Chang:** You wish to know about self-defense. Do not look at much movement and flashy techniques; look at this. [He would just stand there, seeming not to change from the position that he was just in.]
> **EM:** Yes?
> **Chang:** (Laughing.) You did not see it?
> **EM:** No, show me again.
> **Chang:** I will not. You are not ready yet to see.

Nowadays, I know exactly what it was that Chang was trying to show me, because I also show it to *my* students, and they do not see anything, either.

Chang was doing exactly what it said to do in the classics, but at a true internal level, which is the only level at which to do the classics. If, for instance, the classic says that you must "raise the back," and you actually raise your back physically, then you do not know this classic. If it says that you must "round the shoulders," and you physically round the shoulders greatly, then you do not know what this means. If it tells us to "concave the chest" and you physically concave the chest greatly, then you do not know what this means either.

One of Chang's expressions was that we should be like a monkey, "No—like the big monkey," he would say, meaning a gorilla. At that time, I had no idea what he meant, other than to walk around like a monkey! "No, inside," he would say. Modern science now tells us about the "C" back, and the getting of the reptilian brain, and we understand what he meant.

> **Chang:** [Remember, he is answering questions that I have asked regarding self-defense.] You must become like an animal—not like its *movements*, but *inside*. . . . You cannot defend yourself. Only as an animal can you properly defend yourself. We do not have claws, we do not have big, sharp teeth, we do not have strong beaks; it must come from within. Humans are weak; animals are strong.

Chang knew about the reptilian brain but could not relay this information in speaking terms, not even in Chinese, as it is an internal thing that is very difficult to convey to others. When I feel the "back rising" or rather, "the qi rising up the back," I say to people, "See that?"

"No," they reply. Of course they cannot see it. It is happening internally. Chang could feel something great, but it did not manifest itself physically, bar a slight change in body posture. His back would become slightly curved (a "C" back) and his eyes would become slightly crazed like a crazy man. At such times I would not go near him because I knew what the consequences would be.

> **EM:** Who do you think "has" this true internal way of self-defense?

Chang: I do not have ability, but the animal within does. Look at me. Can this old body fight?!

EM: Yes, I have seen and felt it fight.

Chang: Did you see my eyes? It is not me.

This gets back to the fact that it was always his body and internal mind that did the damage and not his conscious mind. Chang was not actually harming anyone; it was his subconscious mind that did the dirty work.

Chang told me that after Yang Shou-hou, no one knew real taiji. Many schools were all physical and would pretend that muscular force and body alignment were internal power. Others would teach no more than a dance, not wishing to get their hands dirty, so to speak, by actually making contact with an attacker.

EM: What will happen to taiji in years to come?

Chang: In the years to follow there will be no taiji, only a shell of movement, with many saying that they are the real masters only to gain fortune. I have seen my art grow smaller and smaller, so that now there are only three that I know of who know the real taiji from Yang Shou-hou. I am teaching you, but I will never know if you will teach yourself from what I have given you. I am too old.

EM: How can I teach myself?

Chang: By just doing it and seeing how I do it. This is the only way. When I was younger, I would see things and would think that I would never know this. My teacher told me that there was no possible way that he could ever teach me the final steps, take me through that final door. So I thought that I would never know. Now, I am in the same position as my teacher, and I feel helpless to show you. I can only hope that what I have shown you already will grow inside and someday, you, too, will know.

Now I am trying to relay that final knowledge to others, trying to find a way where Chang and Yang could not. And, with a superior knowledge of the English language and basic communicating skills, I am having some little success. I think that I learned more from Chang by his just being there and allowing me to "feel," subconsciously, that internal strength and how he caused it to come out.

Chang knew that the self-defense art of taiji was not a physical art but rather a mind art. We learn all of the physical things, which take many years themselves, so that we can have the bodily requirements of a surefooted animal. Then our reptilian brain takes over and does all the rest for us.

Because we are not animals and do not have animal weapons, we must use certain techniques and points on the human body as our weapons. Once we have learned this, we then allow the inner mind to take over and do the rest. We have certain body postures to help us to get into this mode, and we have the learned "ways of doing things" from our forms, katas, kumite, and other two-person training methods, to give us the physical abilities to keep up with what our reptilian brains are trying to have our bodies do.

> **Chang:** If you try to use techniques, then you are being human, and humans cannot fight. Techniques are human things. Dogs do not have techniques, a shark does not have technique, an eagle does not have technique. Only humans have technique. So we are beaten when we have technique. Animals just *be*. They are just doing what they have been told to do. We do what we think we should do. We try to use techniques, and then we lose the ability to adjust the body to what is happening to

it. If we are attacked to the face, we immediately try to cover up using our hands. A dog does not have hands, so it bites our nose. We should make our hands like the dog's mouth; they should bite the attacker's nose off. But we cover up. We do not wish to fight; we are not animals. When we become like an animal, we do what has to be done and don't even think about it afterward. Things happen too fast for technique.

EM: Are there any techniques that you like?

Chang: No. We should not use technique. Have you not been listening? When we use technique, the foot does this, the hand does this, the legs do that, and the body never really moves as a whole. When a dog is attacked by another dog, it does not use its paw to block the oncoming attack, but rather moves its body, not to get away from the attack but to get into a better position to attack the neck! It causes the attack to tell it what to do. If we are continually thinking of doing techniques, then we are only using portions of our bodies, and not the whole body as an animal does. Look at the snake, one from whom I have learned much. You touch it, and it does not move only that portion of its body. The whole body, from head to tail, moves together. Before you know it, it has wrapped itself around your arm, then around your other arm, then it bites you. We should also do this. When we are attacked, the attacker should see that we are there, but when his fist reaches us, we are not there, and we have attacked him instead.

EM: But how do I get to there?

Chang: You do everything that I have shown you, and if you are egoless enough, then it will just come.

EM: What, then, is the most important part of my training?

Chang: It is all important, but at some time, you will find that some parts become more important to you. When you "know" the forms, the fa-jing forms then become more important to you because you do not know them as well. Then as the inner part of you becomes more prominent, you will not wish to practice any more the physical, but you must. At this time you must.

EM: But I see you practice hardly any movements. Is this because you know it all?

Chang: I do not know the internal. You cannot see the internal. It is much more difficult to train than the mere physical. I hear people saying that their teacher practices the pure taiji because he learned it from the son of Yang Cheng-fu, and he must know the correct movements. I hear others say that the posture of "brush the knee" must be done with the hand in such and such a position. These people do not know taiji. They cannot. If they did, then they would not be talking like this. They would know that the ultimate is to become almost purely internal, when there is no or little external movement. At this stage you cannot say if he is doing it better than him, because you cannot see what they are doing.

EM: But surely there is a correct way to do the forms in the beginning?

Chang: Yes. You do it the way that Yang Lu-ch'an did it, like Yang Shou-hou did it. This way you have a better chance of obtaining the internal. There are some people who do not even need any training. They are already internal.

EM: Who?!

Chang: Lao-tze, Buddha, Jesus, and that

man I saw yesterday with the hammer.

I once asked Chang what his ideas on philosophy were, expecting him to come back with some profound sayings from Lao-tze, etc. He said, "See this rock? That is philosophy."

The following Chang Yin-chun interview was my last with Chang. In my final term with Chang, I became adept at phrasing questions so that I would not end up in great pain, and I would ask questions that I needed to know the answers to, as I guess I sensed that he would not be around for much longer.

> **EM:** The way that you do your taiji form is still greatly different to what I am doing, even though I think that I am doing it at the highest level.
> **Chang:** You are doing taiji; I am not. [I was a little worried about this statement. But before I could question him further, he answered me.] Go around to all of the taiji classes. And then come back to me. If you still wish to do taiji, then go and learn from them.

By this stage, I was more than a little confused, but Chang would not be budged on this; no more questions.

I did what he wanted me to, even though I knew what the others were teaching, and then something fell on me. Even though they were doing different styles (Chen, Yang, Wu, etc.), they were all still *doing* taiji. It seemed like an effort, like it was something different that they had to do each day, whereas when Chang did it, it was as if he was not doing anything. He would talk to me while he was doing his form, look around, take in the local scenery, but he was always so still and at peace with everything. He would never actually finish the form, but rather just move into another area of form, like walking to his place of residence or having a cup of tea.

My next visit to Chang was different.

> **EM:** You are not *doing* taiji; you are living taiji.
> **Chang:** No. You are still wrong. I am not living anything; **I am** taiji. You are trying to **do** taiji, so you will never realize the fighting of taiji nor the healing of taiji. You are much stronger than I, and faster, but I seem faster and stronger than you. I am not. I **am** taiji.

From then onward, I tried to *be* taiji with every waking and sleeping moment, as if I were still doing the form. That was his greatest gift to me. To show me to not *do* taiji.

Later, just before he left, Chang told me about the more physical reasons as to why he was not doing taiji. He even said that he would probably not even call his art "taiji," but rather take it back to its original name of "hao ch'uan," which means loose boxing. This, too, came as a big shock, as I thought the name "taijiquan" had been with us from the start. But it has not. Again, if Yang Lu ch'an came back to us now, he would probably want to learn this great new art that had the temerity to take on the name "supreme ultimate boxing." It was Chang who first told me that name has only been with us since the late 1800s (I have read other writings since that confirmed this) and that before that it was called loose boxing. On many of the occasions when we would stay concealed and watch a taiji class, Chang would say, "Look at them—does that look like loose? They are slow and very relaxed, but it is not loose. They move like a box!"

And it was true. They *were* moving like boxes. And that was the most poignant thing that I've ever heard anyone say about anyone else's taiji— *they move like boxes.*

We spend many hours trying to get our bones all moving together, but when Chang did it, it was as if his bones were not connected, but rather, one tiny movement down here would set something in motion up here, and one tiny movement up here would set the whole body into motion, not altogether, but rather a millisecond after that initial movement. And isn't that the way to use fa-jing?

This was the physical difference between my own "hao ch'uan" and his. There were so many little shaking movements—so small that one would perceive only that there was something different. Only once did Chang do the form so that I could see all of the shakes, and that was enough. That was my last lesson with him. Upon which he said—and I use his exact words here—"No need me." He was never at our training spot again.

His muscles were gone. He could not make use of the ground any more, as for this one needs to have physical strength. But he was strong. I was strong then—much stronger and younger than I am now—and yet, I could not match him. I often wonder whether it was just that I was at a low level of training at that time, but I don't think so. And yes, I did try. I was not one for "playing the game" of pleasing the master, which got me into much trouble in my earlier years with other masters.

I know that Chang went back to China, and I would like to think that he is still alive on some mountaintop. But if he were here, I can just hear him saying in Chinese, something like the equivalent of "bullshit!" That's what he was, an "F.C." in the true sense of the word. (For those of you wondering what F.C. means, it's a secret society of martial artists and others who have passed the true test of life! Sorry, can't tell you, it's secret!)

BEHIND EVERY GOOD NONCLASSICAL MARTIAL ARTIST

So many masters and sifus nowadays are trying to cut corners and get there the easy way. Their excuse: "I do nonclassical martial arts." Usually it's an excuse for pure laziness and not wanting to do the hard work necessary to turn a martial art into a survival art.

But take a look at the really good so-called "nonclassical" martial artists, those who seem to have found the way and have long since given up their classical part. Their background is usually steeped in the classical martial arts.

Bruce Lee was the prime example of this. Very few, if any, of his students have ever risen to his level of proficiency and inventiveness. It is my opinion that only Danny Inosanto has ever come close, and he has a classical arnis background (and you can't get any more classical than arnis!). Larry Hartsell has a classical wrestling background. I have seen some of the first Bruce Lee students, who are now into their 50s and do not look very well (overweight, poor skin tone, etc.). They look like old men, while Danny still looks young and strong. They write articles saying they can still take on the best of them with one punch, etc., but they look so sick! Who gives one hair off of one rat's bum if they can still punch at 55 years old? What really matters is if one's martial art has kept one healthy and provided a good life, and whether one is able to help others to good, long, healthy lives.

A martial art is supposed to be an integrated system of self-defense and healing. I guess we have to look back to the days when a martial art was really a family's survival art—used for waging wars, not just fighting one person in a pub or doing battle against someone in the ring with rules and regulations. The head of the family, usually the male, would not know if his family would even *be* there when he returned, while his family would not know if he was coming back that evening. This was the way the Yang family taiji began in China. The Yangs were known as the most feared fighters in all of China, and yet, people nowadays call taiji a dance!

Of course, now most of us do not face life-threatening situations every day of our lives. But the art remains the same, and there is no difference between using the internal systems for health or using them for the fighting art; it's the same energy. In fact, when I give seminars, some people like to break them up into one day for healing and the other day for fighting. However, those who only attend for one day, depending upon their preference, really miss out because the healing and martial arts cannot be broken apart. This is how it used to be, and this is how it should be now.

And isn't self-healing the most important? A proper martial art gives one the ability to beat his opponents by simply outliving them! A style of only punches and kicks cannot do this, whereas classical styles can.

No style? Of course Bruce Lee had a style—a number of classical styles, in fact. Taiji was one of these. These are his basics. It is my opinion that Bruce Lee, if he had lived, would have taken his students back to *his* beginnings and taught *how* he knew, and not *what* he knew. And this is what I think about the classical martial arts (e.g., karate, taiji, kung fu, TKD, etc.)—the basics are contained in the classical forms and katas of these arts. This is where we learn the "body management" so important in turning a basic classical style into a street survival system. You cannot take the classical movements from a form or kata and make up physical reasons for their being. They are not there for that. Try to use technique from a form or kata in a real survival situation and you lose. A good martial art does not teach technique, but rather teaches the *mind* through movement and the body.

The so-called nonclassical stylists who have never done a classical style always say the same things, like why waste time doing so many movements that seem to have no meaning. They also say that rather than do katas, why not do the actual techniques from the forms with a partner. Here, the nonclassical person has lost the whole idea of kata, which stems from his simply not knowing the real meaning of kata. We don't do it to learn techniques! We do it to learn internal body/mind movement. It has nothing to do with learning techniques. If your internal mind does not have it, then *you* do not have it.

You do not learn "internal work" from practicing attack/defense situations with a partner. The survival skills come much later, when you learn all about the no-mind state, eagle vision, reptile brain, and fa-jing. Here, we make use of our own natural movements, different in every body/mind. For instance, the most natural reflex action to a simple attack from the front may be to throw up the hands in front of the face (in fright). So here we turn this movement into a more devastating fa-jing/dim-mak strike. Eventually, this new movement, which is merely a modification of what was always there, becomes the sub-conscious response or reflex action to any type of frontal attack by hand.

If you don't have basics, then you've got nothing! And the classic forms and katas are your basics—they teach you how to move. We don't learn really low stances and exaggerated movements so that we can then use them to fight. It's far from that. We do these katas, which involve much discipline, so that we are able *not* to use them when some real trouble is coming our way. If you see a martial artist who, in a serious scrap, simply knocks someone's head off and leaves, then this is a classical martial artist who has done the basics. However, if you see a martial artist who goes into some sort of low stance and on-guard position, etc., and gets *his* head knocked off, then this is the classical martial artist who has never taken his basics beyond basics.

As we become more and more advanced in our survival skills, we tend to use fewer and fewer techniques, preferring to stick with the tried and proven one or two in order to survive. But it's the years of classical work that give us this ability. In a real situation—and I don't mean the odd drunk at a pub—a half-inch step, balanced, here or there can mean the difference between life or death.

So someone who practices the katas or forms day in and day out does not learn how to fight using those forms or katas. Rather, practicing forms teaches one how to survive using much simpler techniques while always keeping the upper position of hands and feet, in terms of balance. On the other hand, you'll get people who go to a few (or even many) lessons at their local karate or kung fu club and then brag that they know the martial arts. This is the other side of the coin. These people—some of who have been studying for 30 years, even—do not know the martial arts because they have not learned to take their art into a survival realm.

So a martial artist will always make a better streetfighter, provided he has taken his art to a higher level of survival and is aware that all the forms and katas in the world will not make him able to fight. He has to learn how to fight as well as learning his martial art. Conversely, someone who has only learned from a few books or taken a few lessons from a number of different teachers and watched a few Bruce Lee movies will never learn about survival.

It's the classical martial arts that teach us the psychology of the fight, which is no psychology. The difference between winning and losing is 50-percent mind and 50-percent body. If you do not have complete control over your own body and mind, then you have not got it. And you can't get this control watching a few Van Damme movies or learning a few high kicks and fast punches. You have to do the work pertinent to the survival skills you are trying to hone.

Look at what happens in a fight or an attack. If you could slow down the action, you would see footwork and handwork. If you take a look at any good kata or form, you will see this exact foot and handwork, only exaggerated and slowed down. This is to teach the mind to tell the body how to move. When you *are* in a real fighting situation, this will naturally speed up and you will automatically use the same postures, footwork, and handwork that you so painstakingly worked upon for the best part of 10 or 20 years. You don't think about it, of course. It's all there, just like learning to shoot a bow. At first you are all hands, but slowly, the bow becomes a part of you, and your body and mind merge into a whole unit until you finally are able to hit the target many feet away subconsciously. It's the same with the katas and forms. We do not do them to learn technique, but rather subconscious mind and body movement.

One does not have to practice the forms and katas forevermore; only until those movements have become subconscious do you have to practice them. Only in this way, when you are involved in a fight, does your art become so-called nonclassical. I myself am one of the most nonclassical martial artists or survival artists ever when it comes to fighting, but my whole background is in the classical. It is the arduous practice in my early years that holds me in good stead nowadays when I perhaps do not have time to practice three of four forms every day. Now I prefer to spend that time with my children, playing music, painting, writing, teaching them about what I have learned, along with their normal schooling.

But isn't that the irony—that we spend all of this time becoming good at survival, and just when we are getting there, we no longer wish to do it! We grow up and our minds mature; we want to keep out of the way of trouble, avoid fighting like the plague. So perhaps we do the martial arts to not do the martial arts!